Becoming Candii

My True Transgender Story

TS Candii

Cover Design: Eduardo Berretta
Professionally Typeset: Diego Felipe Torres Martinez

ISBN: 9798355023393
Printed in the United States of America

D1714510

Disclaimer

This book is based on a true story and was written to provide information to the readers on the subjects discussed.

It is published with the understanding that the writer, contributing writer, editor, and publisher are not engaged to render any type of psychological, legal, or other kinds of professional advice. It reflects the author's present recollections of experiences over time.

Some names and characteristics have been changed, some events have been compressed, and some dialogue has been recreated.

.

"Detestable is not the one who commits injustice, but the one who does it deliberately."

—Democritus
Ancient Greek Politic

TRANS

From the Latin Trans ("through, beyond")

GENDER

From Latin genus ("kind, sort")

Table of Contents

Introduction

*"You can't teach anybody anything,
only make them realize the answers
are already inside them."*

Galileo Galilei
1564 -1642
Italian astronomer, physicist, and engineer

My name is TS Candii, and that's Candii with two "ii" because I never question myself with the "why."

"Becoming Candii" is about my journey through a traumatic psychophysical transformation that made me who I am today: TS Candii, a proudly transgender woman.

My story is a story like any human being on this planet surviving frustrations to pursue a dream. However, unlike other humans, I was born with an assigned sex opposite to the essence of my true self. Although others considered me a boy, I always felt like a girl.

It is difficult to understand what one suffers when experiencing this differentiation. Our torment begins when we become aware of who we are and what others think we are. It was difficult to tell others who saw me as a boy that I was a girl. It wasn't easy to be accepted. However, despite everything, with great suffering and courage, I learned to accept myself.

What do We Know about Transgender?

"We know much more about how nature shapes sexual orientation, and my view of the science is that nurture does very little, if any, shaping of sexual orientation. We know next to nothing about how people come to feel transgender.

"In some deeper sense, showing brain differences, or finding genetic differences, would not at all be surprising. The big question is how these biological influences shape the felt sense of gender identity.

"How do prenatal sex hormones shape the developing brain circuitry which controls your sense of gender identity? Where is that network? How does it work to make this happen, and how does it map out over time, from early childhood to middle childhood through adolescence and young adulthood? And how does that become different in some people to the sex they were assigned at birth? The answer is: We don't know."

Dr. Qazi Rahman, an academic at the Institute of Psychiatry, King's College London, studies the biology of sexual orientation.

Published in The Guardian, Ian Sample, Science editor Sun 10 Jul 2016

*"For what it's worth: it's never too late
to be whomever you want to be.
I hope you live a life you're proud of,
and, if you find that you're not,
I hope you have the strength to start over."*

— F. Scott Fitzgerald
1896 - 1940
American novelist, essayist, and short story writer

"We are what we believe we are."

— C. S. Lewis
1898 – 1963)
British writer

This is the story of a human being who, like many,
was forced to swim against the tides
and survive the most adverse challenges
to reach the other shore—the shore of a rebirth.

1

Nashville, Tennessee

*"I love Nashville, and I love the South,
but on a professional level,
I had started feeling smothered by the Nashville
way of doing things."*

— Deana Carter
American country music singer-songwriter

Childhood. Playful. Painful.

*"If I were to reduce all my feelings
and their painful conflicts to a single name,
I can think of no other word but: dread.
It was dread, dread, and uncertainty
that I felt in all those hours
of shattered childhood felicity: dread of punishment,
dread of my own conscience,
dread of stirrings in my soul
which I considered forbidden and criminal."*

— Hermann Hesse
1877 - 1962
German-Swiss poet, novelist, and painter

I was born in Nashville and almost murdered there. As sad as it may sound, the place that gave me birth wanted to bury me alive.

I was born on December 6th, 1993, in Nashville, Tennessee. Although my born name was Eric Donnell Whitfield, Jr., it had been impossible for me to be identified by this name. They gave me my father's name then, Eric. But I was never Eric, nor a boy.

When I was born, the nurses looked at my genitalia and said, "It's a boy!" They couldn't be more wrong!

I was the fourth born out of six kids on my mother's side. On my father's side, I was the firstborn, first grandchild out of five on my dad's side.

We can look at "sex" as a biological term. One of which is chromosomes. In terms of gender, these are societal expectations. The pattern for boys is blue, and for girls, it is pink. Gender, in terms of imposed stereotypes, rules that some things are acceptable for men while others are for women.

In my case, I make sure how I present myself to those societies' expectations and how I feel inside are matched.

Although I was born 'male,' it didn't fit my inner self. It didn't match my true spectrum of how I felt and thought with what I needed to be related to.

When I was around three years old, I was just me, without questioning anything about my physical body and authentic self inside me. I played, danced, and sang. I was living free on the inside, unaware or cautious of wrongdoing. What I mean by wrongdoing was that the doctor said I was a male, but I was walking like a female. I just have too much of a heart twist in my walk, or I'm speaking with too much body language, or

I'm simply just living and being free and not knowing that I'm being labeled as "different."

I am a transgender woman. I've been transgender since I was born. That's why I chose to pick up my sister's stuff as soon as I started making choices for myself.

I was not drawn to boy's things, no macho looks like those expected in the southern part of America, but kindness, tender behaviors, and compassion for any living thing. So, the world outside and around me became a recurrent nightmare. Why was there no place in this world for a girl like me?

Anyone can see how the whole woman I am outside of me because that's who I am and who I've always been.

People often think that one day we woke up, looked in the mirror, and decided to be trans. I always felt like a girl. I wanted to do "girl things," dress like a girl and play with girls.

One day, the teacher scolded me severely when she found out I had entered the girls' bathroom. She thought it was a mistake on my part and didn't make a big deal about that. However, I thought she was the wrong one. It was then, at a very young age, that I realized I was different from these other children.

Going out to play, children's rights had been very complicated. Other children, the boys, bullied me a lot for wearing tight clothes like my sisters, instead of baggy clothes, for moving with femininity instead of sullenly like the boys.

I couldn't find a group to play with, a place where my innocence and true self could be accepted. I ended up playing with invisible friends, with pets.

At night, I looked up at the Tennessee sky ablaze with stars and wondered if I had come from one of them. I had heard stories of spaceships, of beings from other planets that had been sighted in the field. I thought that, perhaps, I had come with my extraterrestrial family one night with a sky as starry as that and that they inadvertently returned to our planet at a time that I slipped away unbeknownst to them when I wanted to explore what this planet called "earth" was all about. How could they be if they didn't recognize me and showed me no love but only disgusting rejection?

I began learning what it means to be trans when I went to live for a short time in the small studio apartment where my father lived with my paternal grandmother, a lesbian. She could not understand my father's hideous rejection of his own child for having been born a girl trapped in a boy's body. He already knew about transgender through his lesbian mother. My paternal grandmother started dating women when she was an older person.

My lesbian grandmother had a woman as a partner for about ten years. My grandmother loved me and respected my choice. It was perhaps easy for her to understand because it had also been her choice when she was an older woman: to live with a woman.

My father also knew her mother's story, which was why my paternal grandmother never understood why her son made my life so difficult by wanting to be a transgender woman. What made me precious to my paternal grandmother was that I had been her first granddaughter and my father's first son—the value of the firstborn.

My paternal grandmother was funny and made me feel good. She laughed at her occurrences. She seemed to know how to find a way around life's problems and take them with humor. I learned a lot from that positive behavior. And it wasn't because her life was easy. She struggled, like all of us who lived with limited economic resources. However, the lack of money was not considered "poverty" but simply "lack of money." Poverty was that of the weak and evil spirit.

One day, she was going out because she had a doctor's appointment and let me have one of my gay friends who came to visit me while she was gone. When my dad found out, he went crazy.

She loved me no matter what. Seeing my father's reaction, my grandmother never told him again that she let me have company. She took those secrets to her grave to avoid my father's wrath and how that made me feel.

My grandmother passed away on December 1, World AIDS Day 2016. She suddenly dropped dead. It was unexpected. She was walking out the door with her oxygen tank to receive the new tank a man was bringing her when she felt lifeless. She fell to the floor as if someone in heaven had cut the threads that held her alive. She fell as soon as she opened the door as if she had come to find death knocking on that worn wood of the door.

The man who was going to deliver the oxygen immediately called 911. When I arrived, I saw the ambulance and the police car in front of my grandmother's house. I wanted to run to hug her, but they stopped me. They took her away in the ambulance in an attempt to resuscitate her.

My dad arrived at the hospital and found his mother dead. She had told my father to give me a gold ring that he had given her, which is what my dad did. I have it since then, on my finger. I look at it with love as I write this chapter. It saddens me not to have her hugs, smiles, and encouragement anymore. However, it fills my heart with affection for having received the unconditional love of that magnificent woman, my paternal grandmother.

My head was a puzzle with many missing pieces, and I couldn't find a way to put it all together.

I was curious to learn more about what it means to be "different," to feel different from the sex you received at birth. This enlightened me and helped explain all the problems I had had for as long as I can remember sadness, rejection, unspoken violence, and overt violence.

I don't need to tell people I'm transgender because it's natural for me to "be a woman." It is as if a man born male and feeling that way, or a woman born with female assigned sex and feeling that way, tells everyone they meet: "Look, I'm a man," or "Look, I'm a woman." Because I am a woman, I always felt that way.

I never felt like a boy. I was just forced to live like a boy for the first 12 years of my life.

Trans people are the same as others. We seek to be happy, to be respected, to be free. It is impossible to live in a culture that harasses transgender people and labels them as undesirable beings to society, perverts, and prostitutes.

People openly prejudiced against trans people changed their minds when they understood who I am and how I was born.

There is no real difference between cisgender [non-transgender] people and me. We have dreams too. We are human beings with the right to live openly what we embrace of our authentic being. We have the right to decent work and medical treatment without discrimination. We have the right to study and achieve the best version of ourselves.

The dehumanizing behavior that many people have against us pushes transgender people to live marginalized. And they are left with no choice but to survive through sex work. Many transgender people find suicide the only way out of the deep pain. Society outcasts them by few possibilities to improve their lives, not much support to study, no chances to work, not much help to receive a decent roof, and no medical help. Many die by suicide or have attempted to take off their lives if they have not been killed before by ruthless murderers of transgender people.

Many people believe that one day we woke up and decided to be trans. It is essential to know that it is not a choice. Nothing that had happened in my life had made me trans. I was born trans. I was born "beyond" my assigned sex at birth. And this never made me feel "abnormal" because it was always typical for me to feel like a girl in my childhood and a woman growing up.

When my parents openly heard from my own voice that I was a woman trapped in a man's body, they were outraged. I was 12 years old for 13.

I think that part of their anger towards me was the hidden fears of how this decision to come out as a woman could affect my life in society. Would I be mistreated? Would someone try to kill me? Would I find decent work? Would I become a prostitute? Would I live on the street without a home? Would you find a partner? Could I one day have my own family?

Would I be exposed to the most infernal dangers? Well, YES! A lot of their premonitory panics happened to me. But I survived them.

In Middle school, around eight years old, I loved to wear tight clothing. I loved how my sister's clothes fed, how it was fitted. I didn't like anything loose. I wanted to feel my body. I was not convinced I was behaving wrongly toward my family and those around my environment.

I was wrong for living and being me and so growing up in school, wearing female clothing, a little bit, a hair bow tie, like a little hairband that goes around your head that you put on to keep your hair back or whatever like that. It was like a female hairband and maybe a female shirt. Because a female shirt was always more fitted and tighter, I loved that.

When I was a child, I liked to dress in girl's clothes. I'd sneak out and pull out one of my sisters' clothes, look in the mirror, and flirt, pretending I was walking through a fashion show. I did my hair like my sisters, and I loved putting ornaments on my head. One of my favorite games was playing hide and sought. We called the hidden monster, playing with my friends from school.

Sometimes I feel the unconscious anguish that I found a bathroom. I have dreamed of going to the bathroom, but when I wake up, my bed is wet because I peed on myself. It doesn't happen to me often, but it worries me when it does. Also, in childhood, sometimes I woke up wet. It had been a very traumatic experience because then I would listen to my mother's anger, blaming me for what I had done. I felt embarrassed, too. But it was something I couldn't help.

Growing up, I thought about this and consulted a neurologist, who told me I would have suffered from deep emotional trauma. He did a neurological study to see if there was any disorder in my brain, but he found nothing. He ruled out the neurological factor and concluded they were repressed emotions and unresolved trauma.

I loved that school and studying. I was always excited about the class. One day, I'll never forget my Hispanic teacher, Mr. Santiago, who yelled at me because I was wearing a girl's bow tie. I did not understand why he kicked me out of the class. He asked me to leave and was angry. I was eight years old and perplexed because he embarrassed me in front of the whole class as if I had committed an abominable act. As if by presenting myself as I did, I had offended him and my companions. But I just wanted to wear that bow. What could be wrong with that?

He immediately called my mom and told her I had shown up with a girl's bow on my head, which was disrespectful. My world collapsed. My world of the happy child still didn't realize that I was a girl feeling very feminine, without any awareness that I was trapped in a boy's body.

At home, too, my world was going to end at this point.

My mom became very upset with me. She was embarrassed when the teacher called again to find out what I was wearing another female object.

I imagine it must have been evident to my mother that I was a girl born in a boy's body, but she had never said anything to me or asked me how I felt. And I felt normal. All was well in my world. I had access to girl stuff through my sisters, and it seemed like nothing was wrong with me playing with their girl toys and wanting to wear their clothes too.

However, that incident at school transformed my mother. She told me that I couldn't be me." It was forbidden for me to wear feminine clothes. It was incorrect; it was not normal to feel how I felt. Everything returned to me like a landslide, and I would fall into a terrifying abyss. What was not normal? Wasn't I a girl?

To make matters worse, not only the prohibition of expressing myself as I hurt me deeply, but also the tone that my mother used in her attempt to destroy the girl in me. There were no sweet words for my tears. No support for my Suddenly, I looked around, and everyone looked at me as it judging me. Where did those cold gazes come from? What? I thought they were my siblings. It seemed that the joy had gone numb.

My mother's rejection felt like contempt for me. I shook myself into inconsolable tears, but no one hugged me to ease the pain of suddenly feeling cut off from the only thing I knew and loved: my mother, my father, my siblings, and my home. There was no loving support, no kind words, no understanding of what I felt; there was nothing to hold me while I was falling apart. I was shaking and crying. And I was only eight years old.

I thought this made sense. I grew up in hostile environments where verbal and physical violence, and even the violence of rejection, alert me to react to any situation that could put my life in danger.

Yes, of course, which children are not afraid? Children can be frightened of the dark and other things we imagine as monsters hiding under the bed or in the closet. What terrified me the most was asking, "Who would embrace me when I needed a hug? Who would protect me if something terrible happened to me?

It was clear that in my world, as a sensitive girl, I perceived rejection as something that, at any moment, could expose me to mortal danger. And when that happened, no one would be there to protect me.

Another thing I found meaning in sometimes wetting the bed after dreaming that I'm going to a bathroom, or even my anguish about finding a bathroom, has to do with my gender identity. I feel like a whole woman, yet I have to go to the men's bathroom with all the distress it produces to me.

My childhood was challenging. Imagine how it feels when in the early days, the child is being labeled as a monster, the shame of the family. A shame for my father's firstborn child. A shame for my mother. I was growing up like how to deal with those who wanted me to be a boy, play like a boy, dress like a boy, and behave like a boy when I WAS NOT. I grew up TERRIFIED of being myself. I grew up hearing the worst things a child could hear from parents.

Looking back, I am blessed that I didn't kill myself, although, somewhere in their hidden minds, my family would want me to vanish from their lives. They didn't want to show that this monster came from my parent's genes. They even wished to abort me if they would ever suspect the "kind" of being they brought to this world.

I don't know where I got the strength to face the horror of the environment that rejected me and wanted me to be dead. I grew up terrified of people finding out because I had no idea what was happening inside me. It was hard to understand why they hated me so severely. I was alone, without anyone like me to relate to. To feel I am 'normal.' It seemed that for "the others," I was a threat. A devil. A poison ivy. Mentally ill.

I was longing for a miracle. A physical transformation that would match my true self. But I didn't have a clue about my possibilities. I didn't know anything about hormones and surgery procedures. So, I try to hide my little girl from harm, abusive words, physical abuse, and possible death by being murdered. However, I was clueless about what part of me I should hide, as everything in me seemed normal despite the outside world's reactions. I didn't understand what gender meant. There was a time when I brought anger and some aggression against myself for having been born this way—a misunderstood girl who couldn't find a way to be beloved since my very early days.

Not everyone in my family turned their back on me in some way. There was a being; I would say an angel, who brought blessings to all who knew him just with his magnificently kind presence. He was my maternal grandfather, and his name was Howard Brown. He had one of the most compassionate spirits I have ever met. Whenever he saw me, he would open his arms and comfort me with his generosity without judging me. He never paid attention to any way of discriminating against a human being. For him, I was his granddaughter, a human being hungry for affection and respect and in great need of support to help me make my trans journey as painless as possible.

Thanks to him, I was accepted into the church, where he participated generously. That church welcomed me without judging me. I grew up there and became the choir director for children and youth. However, one day, a somewhat expected but still painful day, we voted for the new pastor after the previous one had passed away. This new pastor (a man who preached God's love, kindness, compassion, generosity, and godly behavior) took me one day to his office and told me that I could no longer lead the church choir because he didn't want his son to grow up like me.

I was sorrowful. I knew that my life had never been a choice. I knew very well that I had not chosen to feel like a girl, a woman. I WAS. I also knew that what was happening to me was not contagious. It is difficult to understand how transgender people feel if someone does not have an open, humanitarian, understanding spirit in the face of what is different.

When I told my beloved grandfather, he smiled softly at me to prevent tears from appearing in his sad eyes. Then, he stroked my head and told me, "Your spirit is pure. You have nothing to be ashamed of—no one on earth with the divine authority to judge another human being. Trust in who you are and pray to the Lord to help you. We all know the suffering of being considered unwanted and discriminated against.

The world doesn't need more sadness caused by those who hate the "different." The Lord, in this immense love, will always protect you. And I will continue to pray for you." He then got up from this porch chair and said, "Come child, let's walk and listen to the birds, listen to the wind whispering through the branches. Let's breathe what is pure in life. Nature, in its wisdom, knows how to relieve a troubled mind. People do not have an answer for everything. A compassionate heart does not ask, just love, which is the answer God wants us to give to all questions: "love your neighbor as yourself."

He never made me feel abandoned. When I lived in Nashville, Tennessee as a store manager, I used to stand at the bus stop and wait for the bus. My granddad was passing by driving this gray pickup, stopped as soon as he saw me, and gave me a ride to work. He told me he worked as a security officer overnight at the same mall. I went to work that day with a broad smile, and people asked me later if I had won the lottery. I responded, "Yes. My granddad is the best reward anyone can dream of having in life."

My grandfather told me that when my great-great-grandmother married our slave-owning brother, we had sort of little children in a school, a store, and a church, where many of our family members were buried in the back. Years later, the school burned down, then the store burned down, and more recently, the church burned down. He told me he remembered going to the cemetery to visit those who had preceded him. I imagined him as a child visiting his deceased ancestors, and even when he was little, my grandfather's compassionate and noble spirit was already manifested.

Unfortunately, he passed due to Covid in 2020. There were trees planted in his memory. It was a significant loss to the family and the community when he departed. I know those trees will extend their branches to heaven to say hello and thanks to my grandfather. I know his spirit would walk around nature, still grateful for the wisdom he learned from it.

Life, the years, did their work and narrowed the gap between my parents and me. In their own way and time, they learned to value, respect, and love me as I am, as I always was, a woman trapped in a man's body.

It has brought peace to my heart to know that reconciliation between my parents and me has been achieved. I had always loved them. I never had it in my early years; however, I survived.

I communicate with my mom every day and my dad every two weeks. The two have been separated for many years. They are still young, and I am glad they have found a way to heal and forgive themselves through my forgiveness.

There is no resentment or incrimination towards them for abandoning me to my fate when I needed them most. Instead, I was thrown out of the street and sentenced at age thirteen to start prostitution as a means of survival. I might have had a guardian angel to be here, healed, an achiever transgender woman, telling you my story now at 28.

I don't blame them. I never blamed my mother or father for not wanting to hug their male-born daughter. They were perhaps too young and full of prejudices. They sought refuge in religion to ease the difficulties of poverty in our modest home in Nashville, Tennessee. But faith was the first to censure me for not wanting to accept behaving according to the sex assigned to me at birth. And my mother thought that I could have come as a curse to the family, and indeed, my father thought the same.

Surviving Suicidal Desires

"But, in the end, one needs more courage to live than to kill himself."

— Albert Camus
1913 -1960
French philosopher, author, dramatist, and journalist

Surviving hell and going back to hell is not surviving at all.

It is harsh to be transgender and live in a society like any other human being. As if we were a scourge, we are pushed into the abysses of the underworld. Once there, we are chased by those who clean the cities of the "unwanted people." The underworld also has its rules. It has the law of the stronger that massacre the weak after abusing their power over the most vulnerable or the less lucky.

Many of us do not see life options in these conditions. So, we chose to take our lives. And we intended to do so as many times until we succeed. That is, stop breathing because the life society conditions us to live becomes mere existence. An existence without hope of evolving, of progressing, of having a job, a decent roof, a family, and medical attention.

I have wondered if the desire to commit suicide was part of a self-preservation instinct. Not preservation of life, but the instinct to avoid constant tortures and unbearable suffering. Preservation of that deep emotional pain that only a total numbing of the mind could calm.

The constant torment, ruthless discrimination, and inhumanity of many make the right to life impossible. The escape route heads to suicide.

Some managed to die trying to kill themselves, and others were rescued. However, suicidal thoughts continue to accompany transgender people like a friend who comes, listens to us, and comforts us—death as a faithful friend who comes to rescue us from deep emotional pain. But when we fail to die through a self-inflicted attempt, we have more options: keep trying or ask for help.

There were times when I was suicidal, especially as a child. When arguing with my brother, I would sometimes take a knife and put it to my heart as if doing so, I would remove the poison received from humiliating insults and other aggression within my family, at school, and on the street. Everywhere.

After several suicidal attempts, I asked for help. It was when a new me came out. If I cannot self-destruct myself, I will try to reconstruct myself.

Social constructions of gender, including binary concepts and stereotypes about sexuality in many cultures, perpetuate stigma, discrimination, transphobia, and violence in all its forms against trans people.

Being different should not be considered a disorder or illness. Being a trans person is not a disease, and it is not a choice.

The new International Classification of Diseases (ICD-11) no longer defines transgender identity as a psychological problem or as a mental disorder, as it was a few years ago.

Social exclusion for those born transgender often begins early within the family. Discrimination in schools and health systems continues. Subsequently, they are prevented from easy access to education, employment, social protection, and social participation. These barriers prevent trans people from receiving the proper health services for their care and treatment.

Many times, the first oppressors of trans children are their parents. Parents who, instead of accompanying them, educate themselves about what happens to their trans children choose to harass them. They prefer to hide them or throw them out of their homes as if instead of having a child, they had spawned a monster or a baby possessed by the devil that had to be exorcised. Parents who bully their children end up pushing them to suicide or to seek escape in underworlds where crime, prostitution, youth trafficking, and drugs live.

Discrimination and criminalization are the cause of many hate crimes and suicides.

Every person has the right to have their legal identity recognized. The legal recognition of trans people is relevant considering that the possibility of identification, consistent with the expression of the gender of trans people, allows access to education, health services, justice, work, and particularly the exercise of all her rights as any citizen, including the right to vote.

For the life expectancy of trans women to approach that of the general population, it is necessary to fight against stigma, ensure access to health and heal the wounds that discrimination has opened in transgender people to allow them to live with the joy of embracing the right to whom we feel we are. The life expectancy of transgender women ranges between 35 and 42 years, while the general life expectancy is 75 years. This is exacerbated in black trans women.

Being expelled and not integrated into society is a particular death sentence—self-inflicted death by suicide to escape the horror of life or death caused by intolerance and inhuman behaviors.

The risk of suicide and suicide attempts is roughly three times higher than that of the rest of the cis population, and that suicide is the third leading cause of death among adolescents in the United States of all types.

The discharge of violence against trans people is a first-level justice and public health problem. It is inhumanely a particularly vulnerable and persecuted group, still not respected by many societies.

Even today, dozens of European countries require sterilization to recognize the identity of trans people, with the medical risks that this indicates and the ignorance of the trans nature since many of them do not feel dysmorphophobia, a disorder that produces the fear that one's own body, or any part of it, is or may become repulsive, or want to have surgery.

Being trans is daring to walk through a minefield only for the right to inhabit our true selves. We never know, or can know, when the next step will take us to certain death, or we will continue on the path of being what we feel and recognize ourselves to be.

We, trans people, are accused of something we have not done. We are not criminals, nor want to be out of the law.

We have problems finding work, having a roof sheltering us, problems achieving school inclusion, the right to be healthy, the right to be healed when we don't feel well, and we are exposed to dangerous and stressful street harassment. Many receive death threats or torture and violent attacks.

The petty, ruthless, and ignorant poverty of a society with a phobia of transgender people condemns them to absolute poverty, with a lack of money, food, shelter, and health care without feeling the honor of being a human being. So, too many transgender people die from physical debilitation and emotional deterioration.

The highest degree of social discrimination is recorded in primary and secondary school. Trans people are verbally abused with disqualifying names and physical attacks that make them want to drop out of school to avoid exposure to emotional and physical wear traumas. Many trans people do not go beyond the initial levels of education.

Many trans are thrown out of their homes. Others flee to escape the violence unleashed against them within the family and at school. Most ends in the street at 12 or 13 years old, and young trans women are forced into sex work to pay for food or shelter.

These days I want to live. I do not seek to make myself disappear from the scene of life as I tried so many times when I was a child, a teenager, and in my early twenties.

Now that I have managed to inhabit a female body after tremendous tribulations, physical and mental pain, fears, and deep sadness, now that I have reached my goal, I want to travel. I would like to be an experiential part of our world. I would like to know about other cultures. I would like to love and to be loved.

Triple Rape and Murder:
I Survived Them

*"You are not the darkness you endured.
You are the light that refused to surrender."*

— John Mark Green
American Author

The day I left home, it was a cold winter, and it had heavily snowed. My heart had become so cold that not even its beating knocked on the door inside me. I was standing there, numb, standing on the threshold that would take me to the other shore, and yet I was not sure of my destination.

My mother told me to get my butt up, get out of the house, and get my life on my own. There was a taxi waiting. I had packed my few belongings and was wrapped in sadness, uncertainty, helplessness, and anger. I was being thrown out of my nest.

Although in my nest, I felt like a bird of another species. My family was a different kind of bird than me. They made me feel like I was a black crow and were the thrushes in the Garden of Eden. Years later, I learned about the magnificent intelligence of ravens. Their intelligence is comparable to that of chimpanzees and apes.

I still did not know at that young age of 13 years about the intelligence and wisdom with which I had been gifted and that I would train in the days of survival that would await me later to choose the best strategies to survive all the hell for which I would walk.

Going back to the morning of my 13 years, still, a child, when I was kicked out of my home, it had snowed mercilessly outside. There were like four inches of snow outside.

The merciless cold of abandonment ran through my veins, and I was shaking. I felt like some young animals, abandoned by their mothers because they were considered disposable, with no chance of survival, to their fate. They are being left behind from the herd to be eaten by wolves and bears or to succumb to the terrifying cold of winter.

In that emotional state, I stood at the door, waiting for the taxi to come down the street. The road from the street to the house was extended and blanketed by thick, impassable snow. Due to this great distance between the door and the street, all I could see was when the taxi turned into the driveway.

The distance and road conditions were so great that it would take a long time for the taxi to reach the door. I didn't want my mother to yell at me even more impatiently. I sat on my little suitcase in the doorway as I listened to my mother scream from inside, "I wish I had aborted you," and other things to which my ears closed to listen while my tears fell on my cheeks, already numb from the cold.

Suddenly, she came at me with brutal fury and a plastic broom in her hand, trying to hit me with it. But I caught the broom in an instinctive reaction of not accepting more physical damage, and the broom broke in half. This moment was etched in my memory as a rupture towards what I did not want to belong to either, since I had never been considered part of that family nest.

I took my bag and a small suitcase, ran through the deep snow, got to the taxi, panting, agitated, distressed, and gave him the address of the apartment where my dad lived with my paternal grandmother.

I couldn't help but look out the taxi's back window at what I was leaving behind. My mother was still signing angry, and I'm sure still cursing the day I was born.

My parents were Americans, descendants of several generations of enslaved Africans. There was always pride in all of us for being black. Years later, I learned that my great-great-grandmother had married the brother of a white man who owned considerable estates in the South.

When I heard this story, I imagined how beautiful she would have been and indeed blessed in times of cruel and "accepted" hostility towards the enslaved Black people in the Southern states. She was allowed to marry a man of another social caste. This story seemed so romantic that it nourished my romantic spirit from a dream. The dream was that it would be possible for me too. One day, I might have a family with a man who loves me and recognizes me as a woman even though I am different.

My mom and dad were in a relationship, and a few years after I was born, my mom taught my dad how to drive and fill out applications. It was not a good union for her that gave my father so much. He ended up cheating on her for another woman he had gotten pregnant. That ended the relationship between them. I have concise memories of lying on my father's chest when I was tiny.

The echoes of his fights and screams filled with words I still didn't understand boggled my mind. I loved them both. This violence made me feel threatened that, at some point, I would be left without my father or mother.

Living with my father and paternal grandmother was not as easy as I imagined. The studio apartment was too small for three people to live in.

Only my paternal grandmother accepted me in that place, and I think her understanding came from the world in which she had already chosen to live as a flattering woman, as a lesbian. So transgender life was not deplorable for her. However, it was intolerable for my father. Over the years, my father and I achieved a good relationship.

It took years for my father to finally understand that my decision was not a whim or a choice. I had always been a woman caged in the body of a man.

I always defended my rights despite the cruelty of the world against me. Despite the abuse, humiliation, and life threats, I had to endure it. I even had to accept being left out of school in ninth grade because of the brutal intolerance I received, even though I was an excellent student and loved studying and learning.

Going back to that pivotal time of my life, when I was thirteen years old, I suffered for the first time not only the terrible physical and emotional pain inflicted on me but also became too close to a violent death experience.

It all started when I was sitting in a park one afternoon in Nashville, Tennessee. It was summer, and that weather made me feel joyful. I started appreciating the beauty of nature and how blessed I was to witness life miracles. I remember a smile comforting me just for being there in that calmness.

Even when there was a small muddy pond, greenish from the floating verdigris, I was glad to see the ducks swimming in pairs as if such dirty water was not something to consider. I thought about how beautiful nature was and that it did not have discriminating behaviors towards things that we humans could consider undesirable.

Although at that early age, my mind could discern what the culture believed to mistreat those considered different. Cultural cruelty was already installed in the minds of the little ones, the kids, to inflict perverse treatment on other children considered "outcasts" by society.

I felt lonely. Not only alone sitting on that bench, but in the immense loneliness felt by someone who has no one to talk to, with whom to share the true self. The loneliness of not having anyone who would hug me or comfort me in moments of deep despair.

I entertained myself by looking at those ducks rushing toward a lady standing in the distance. She was throwing breadcrumbs at them, so they would run to their side, fluttering to get more morsels.

Other people came and went, just as the branches moved from one side to the other in the rhythm of the breeze that passed through them. I smiled for a moment, imagining some trees acting on a stage, moving their branches full of leaves as if hiding from the rhythm of the fans they moved. I always imagined scenes on set in the theater and dreamed of them as musicals. Artists, dancing and singing happy and inspiring songs.

Suddenly something interrupted the calm of that thoughtful and peaceful moment. I saw someone I used to know approaching me. A man who unexpectedly and when no one was around caught me off guard, put a bag over my head, and dragged me into some tall bushes, helped by two others who prevented me from moving.

I tried to defend myself as much as I could. I had the strength to do it, but they were three men, and they were talking to each other, cursing me, and laughing.

They threw me on the ground and, one after another, violently raped me. I could hardly breathe, but I tried to put my teeth every time the bag came closer to my mouth on each inhalation to break it and get air. In my despair, all the physical pain I felt was likely numbed by the extreme stress I was under. Nobody had ever penetrated me. My physical body had never received such violence.

Despite everything, I did not want to die. I tried to fight for my life. My whole being told me that I had to overcome this moment of violation physically, mentally, emotionally, and spiritually.

When they finished mistreating me impiously, with my hands partially tied and the plastic bag still on my head, they threw me into the water, so I would die without any chance of saving myself.

But my survival instinct, my angels, the spirits of my ancestors, and God gave me the energy, the power to swim. I only had in mind that I would make it to shore anyway, while muddy, putrid water seeped a little into my mouth and nose through the bag parts I had broken with my teeth.

The ducks swam away from me without understanding what animal was swimming near them. With the force of my desperation, I managed to swim and get out of the water.

The woman who had been throwing breadcrumbs to the ducks rushed to my aid and helped untie my wrists. I was crying uncontrollably. I was terrified. I was all wet, bathed in disgusting mud and blood. I had survived a horrible death.

They would have found me floating like a corpse in the filthy water, and no one would have ever found out who the criminals were. I would have relieved my family, who didn't want to know anything more about me if I had died. However, having died after a triple rape and drowning would indeed have left my parents with a terrible pang of conscience.

The woman said to call 911, but I was in such a state of physical and emotional deterioration that I just wanted to go to my mom's house. I barely understood the shock I was in. The trauma I was carrying while trying to walk to get to the home I had been kicked out of. I needed to go there in desperation because I was still a child, and it was all I had ever known.

When I arrived at my mom's house, she greeted me with a sixth sense that made her behave compassionately when she saw me in such a deteriorating condition. I could barely walk. She prepared the shower for me. Then I went to bed shivering. I couldn't tell her immediately because I didn't know how to digest it myself. I found it hard to believe that this had been a harrowing experience and not just a nightmare created by the mind. How would those men be such devilry to me, a kid? Even wanting to murder me?

My mom respected my silence. There were gestures of tenderness in her that I never knew in my life as a child. She covered me with a blanket and kissed my feverish forehead. I slept. I slept for many hours.

When I recalled that traumatic experience, I wondered, how can such demonic beings consider themselves human, outraging a child's life? How can they live with themselves, their consciousness? Do they perhaps have human consciousness, divine? I do not think so.

I later gathered energy and told my mom what happened to me. She hugged me and cried. She then began to curse those men. To curse also the life I would lead, exposed to all kinds of physical and emotional insults. She told me that if I insisted on my decision to be the woman my body had not given me, I could end up receiving a horrible death. I was heartbroken, non-stop crying.

My mother told me that my life was saved by a miracle this time, but who knows if I would survive another attack. She kept screaming with her arms raised and cursing at those criminals. She then looked at me again and hugged me again.

We immediately went to the police to file a complaint since I knew the promoter of my rape and attempted murder. They took my statement while looking at me out of the corner of their eyes, perhaps wondering how, after such an attack, I was still alive. I was still there, so young and with the guts to denounce those criminals. He was then about twenty-eight years old, and his two friends of his were perhaps the same age. They were men, and I was a small, frail thirteen-year-old girl.

After a while, we were in court. I remember that the judge made everyone leave the courtroom because I was a minor. He wanted to prevent my intricate outrage from being heard by a large audience. I appreciated what he did because I felt protected and safe.

Seeing them again in court brought to my mouth the disgusting taste of that putrid water. The rapist and his henchmen were arrested. I never knew anything if they were sentenced and ended up in a penitentiary. I was a child and did not understand much of what was happening. The only thing I knew very well was that my body had been terribly mistreated by those abominable men, who fled calmly with their lives because they thought I had drowned in that nasty pond.

My father and mother separated when I was still a child. He had financial difficulties supporting himself and went to live in the small studio apartment with his mother, my paternal grandmother, who chose to be openly lesbian and older. Around the age of 14, I had no choice but to go live with them, despite being all very cramped in that shoebox where they both lived.

Since I trusted my paternal grandmother, and she accepted me as I was, I told her one day that I wanted to get my navel and tongue pierced, to which she replied that she should consult my father. I went to the kitchen, where he was preparing something to eat, and as soon as he heard my wish, he yelled at me and replied that he would disown me if he pierced my tongue or navel.

Around that time, I became defiant before those who wanted me to dress like someone I am not, to behave like someone I am not, or to hide. I had to go to the school to talk to the counselors, whom all felt I needed advice. I heard that I would have to go to treatment for my mental illness, and I also needed to pray a lot for God to free me from the demons that I had in my being. I wondered why I needed treatment or exorcism if it was just how I felt I had to be. But, for the rest who couldn't or didn't want to understand me, the label of mental illness would give them peace of mind and even the possibility of social acceptance also included in that package.

Realizing that I would never have support and, worse, receiving contempt for choosing to be myself, although still very young, I decided to leave. I needed to dress like a woman. I had to embrace who I was and not whom others wanted to force me to be.

I went to big brother and big sister, a non-profit organization, to help young people. It was a good show for about four to six weeks as they tried it out in Tennessee, where they tried to heal families by doing mother-child counseling.

The counselor would try to ensure that the child could return home and live in an environment that guaranteed him safety and prevented him from hostility, violence, and abuse from adults.

Every organization I went to, including Oasis, a rehab center in Nashville, Tennessee, specializes in treating alcoholism, opioid addiction, substance abuse, and mental health and substance abuse, including programs for adults, LGBTQ, men, women, and young adults. They tried to get the young runaway back through weekly counseling sessions.

Many times, the parents and the child attended to be helped. All were trying to make peace so that the young man could return to a healthy environment for the kids at home.

Life and dead:
Those who once lived,
where did they go?

"Death is the wish of some, the relief of many,
and the end of all."

—Lucius Seneca
4 BC - 65 AD
Roman Stoic philosopher

As mysterious as it might seem, I always felt comfortable walking and sitting in cemeteries. I wondered where the dreams of those buried there had gone.

The place felt like I was visiting immortality. Where there was nothing before nor after, except a continuous time without life or death to imprison it. There were moments when I also felt immortal. I felt that what dwells in me is an eternal spirit. A traveler of infinity who knows the secrets of life and death yet, cannot find human words to express them.

And those who lie here? Where have they gone? Would there be hell and paradise? Neither? Would this

53

life be hell, and heaven is reached when we go hereafter?

Cemeteries never scared me. On the contrary, I felt drawn to their peaceful atmosphere. Walking among the silenced voices made gave me peace. Would their souls find it?

At a very young age, I discovered that although suffering is part of human nature, as a transgender woman, the psychophysical suffering is magnified to infinite levels. Lacking finding a way out, many of us seek to commit suicide.

Behind the scenes of life, those who departed will go to that place of nothingness where there are no human forms; in fact, the wandering spirits do not bother each other. Unlike in this part of the stage, where we meet those who love to satisfy their sadistic pleasure against the weak. Vile people, who unload on us, the different, the outcast, the undesirable, violence that encompasses both the physical, the curses, and even indifference.

We, the marginalized, live on constant alert, aware of the danger that at any moment and any place, we would be beaten to death, mentally and physically abused even by those who claim to be the law.

I didn't know if cemeteries whispered stories from the other side when the breeze moved the branches, and the leaves blew unheard messages from beyond. All I knew was that among the graves, I felt safe.

One day, after profound desolation, I went to see a psychic. She was a woman endowed with the power of clairvoyance who received messages from the beyond through her remarkable mediumship.

I was anxious to know my transition path until I could manifest the woman in me on the outside. She looked at me, and her gaze showed me a traveler from infinity. Her honey-colored eyes contrasted with her dark pupils. She took a few drags on her already spent and chewed Cuban cigar, shot a dense white smoke upwards, and it was the last thing I remembered. I passed out on a colorful mat she had prepared for that purpose, and I lay there flowing on a shamanic journey.

When I opened my eyes very slowly, I saw a fan of colorful feathers fanning the smoke of incense and sage that she had lit. Faint sunlight filtered through her orange and green curtains, and the smell showered blessings over me.

I asked her what had happened to me, and she told me she needed me to go into a hypnotic trance with her to make a trip to the dimensions where everything was pre-written.

"Although our pre-written life, choices are yours. And this makes you responsible for your decisions," she said, putting her right hand on my shoulder and a wide white smile.

She told me that I would succeed. Ultimately, all my struggles will have been worth it, and I will lead a liberation movement for marginalized beings.

I felt empowered by her words. My terrors seemed to dissipate at her favorable auspices; however, exciting anxiety also pulsed through my veins. She added that a spiritual answer for which I did not die when those three men raped me at the age of 13 and survived suffocation and trauma was precisely for me to be part of the movement that would activate the awakening of social consciousness about the criminalization to which transgender people are subjected.

I wondered if her prophecy wouldn't be too much of a burden for a very young girl whose life had been impoverished by humiliation, contempt, and denigration.

Then fatigue weighed on my eyelids, and I fell asleep. At that time, I was about 14 years old, and on the one hand, my spirit, inspired by the courage, was fighting with the other terrifying part of my being. I woke up sometime later; I don't know how long I could have slept, but she was gone.

Another woman, a transgender woman, a friend of the sorceress, told me that it would be good for me to start hanging out with transgender groups and suggested that I attend a transgender festival in Nashville. However, even being very young and suffering from the outrages of my identity, I heard my call.

My Initiation in Sex Work

*"Eros and Ananke [Love and Necessity]
have become the parents of human civilization."*

— Sigmund Freud
1856 1939
Austrian Neurologist, founder of Psychoanalysis

I met Ashanti when I attended an LGBT event in Nashville, Tennessee. I needed to feel part of a community where I could feel myself, even though I didn't fully understand what was happening to me.

The closest experience I had with those considered "different" was through my lesbian grandmother when I was 14 years old. I got there because I was always kicked out of my home and didn't want to live on the streets.

I arrived at the LGBT event looking for people with whom I could identify and not be a toad from another well, as my family had always made me feel. Even though I discovered that my paternal grandmother was a lesbian when I lived in her house at 14, my mother only found it out six years later. At the gay event, I saw people who looked like me, who acted as I did. They were all friendly and seemed happy in their joy. I felt welcome in their group.

Ashanti was a professional sex worker with a good eye for newcomers to be trained and approached me with a gentle smile. When she found me, after a brief talk, she gave me her phone number and told me she could help me.

I soon called her and went to her house. She welcomed me as if I had always been part of her family and said, "You reminded me of me when I was your age," while she patted me on the shoulder.

I smiled with tears. I sobbed and shared how much I had suffered from my family's disregard and the school. I had no one to relate to. I also told Ashanti, still somewhat shyly, about the rape and attempted murder I suffered two years ago and how I had miraculously survived.

Ashanti made me sit in a comfortable chair across from hers and served me tea with milk and cookies, "Or do you prefer an iced tea?" Her smile was as sweet as those cookies.

I responded that tea with milk was a great idea and ate some cookies, pretending she wasn't starving.

"Come on," Ashanti told me lovingly, "I went through the same thing as you. I know how challenging it is to emerge from your true self with the world sees you differently. But then, you must know that everything will turn out for the best. I'm not saying it's easy. I just say it's not impossible."

I watched her as I gently chewed on the cookies, enjoying each bite as if it might be her last. She then got up with her gentle manners and asked me to come another day.

Before saying goodbye, she asked me if I would be willing to be initiated into sex work. And when I naively asked her what she had to do, she shrugged and said, "the same thing you do with other men, but in this case, you get paid. Do you understand me? You get money. Cash!"

When I saw her again, she received me as if I had walked inside the Dior house. There was a whole wardrobe ready for me to try on clothes in my size. There were fine girl clothes, casual, dress-up, very feminine, and sensual lingerie, and there was also the so-called "neutral clothing."

Ashanti introduced me to roadside sex right away.

She taught me how to protect myself—how to use condoms so that my sex work would start doing oral sex with men, and how to put a price on my work. She let me know she perceived that I had good instincts to screen a client, which gave me confidence. I was 15 years old, and I was brave. I had no choice but to summon my courage to navigate the dark routes of sex work.

My first outfit as a sex worker was a blue jean miniskirt, a pair of boots with heels, a low-cut black faux leather jacket, and a sports bra to show off my small boobs underneath it. Yes, my male body had developed small feminine breasts that I liked to accentuate.

About the oral sex, I had no idea how to do it. Ashanti looked surprised and said, "Really?" Then, laughing took a sausage out of her fridge and sucked on it. It didn't seem to be a tricky thing. And if I would be paid well to imagine that I was sucking on a sausage, all the better.

In my first experience, I was a girl. Just a girl. I did not want to judge who asked me to perform oral sex on him, but an older man stopped his car on the side of the road. He turned off the lights, and I knew it was an invitation to go there.

After doing it, I thought, "Oh, this was easy, and he would pay me for what I did." If only he knew that in my mind, I thought only of the sausage I had practiced with all the time. Of course, that thought came from the little and inexperienced girl I was. When I look back at that moment, I feel disgusted by the adult man who took advantage of my need to abuse an innocent 15-year-old girl.

Getting into the cars or trucks that stop on the road is an adventure that can make us end up in a hospital or the morgue. The other alternative was to starve.

Sex Work vs. Sex Love

"Sex is always about emotions.
Good sex is about free emotions;
bad sex is about blocked emotions."

— Deepak Chopra
Indian American author and alternative medicine advocate

After surviving the terrible rape those three evil men inflicted on me, I was no longer afraid to be with a man.

Sometime later, I found out that the case of my rapists had been dismissed. Of course, it hurt me that they had not been incriminated or judged and that justice had not been done. They not only brutally raped me when I was just 13 years old, but with my head wrapped in plastic and my hands tied, they threw me into the pond full of mud and moss so that I would die there.

Still, there is something in the nature of my inner "being" that has always made me harbor no hatred or resentment. I learned to accept what I cannot change. And what I can change, I will always fight to achieve.

One of the requirements to be a survivor "with a healthy emotional life" is: "discipline," another is "not to feel sorry for oneself," and another essential "is to have a clear objective in life" about the direction that we want this one to have so that it is a life worth living and also a life that helps inspire others to overcome challenges, even the most terrifying ones. As many survivors have done to continue with their lives along prosperous, healthy, fulfilling paths.

Before my sex experience, the first time I fell in love, I was 16 and stayed in a relationship with a man for about two years. His company made me feel all the woman I was. I discovered how romantic I could be with the right guy.

My first love experience was full of romance. Next to him, I felt my feminine world emerge through the pores of my skin.

As I learned later that love is one of the most challenging relationships for anyone in the world, I understood why I have been in love once and in only one stable relationship. He was my first love, and I was fresh, romantic, naive, and too young.

The union lasted for a couple of years until circumstances of our social instability caused weariness, disappointment, frustration, blame, and fights. All those negative feelings that sometimes come to couples who do not have the maturity to detach themselves from external challenges and take refuge in the care of love.

I still remember him today as someone who made it possible for me to heal my wounds from being harshly rejected by my family.

When I was with him, there was no desire to commit suicide. I wanted to live, love, and be loved. Everything was safe. His love sustained me and lifted me above the dangers we transgender people walk through every day.

I feel that my capacity to love is enormous, and it does me good to share my emotions with those who can appreciate them.

Now that my parents have understood who I am, they see me transformed from the outside into the woman I always felt lived in me. The love that circulates between my parents and me is beautiful, healing, restorative, and comforting.

Although I love to expand my feelings among black people, I also enjoy being part of the multi-ethnic cultural diversity I experienced. It also makes me thrilled to love animals. I love everything that lives in nature: birds, wild and farm animals, plants, trees, and people.

But working for sex doesn't include love. When I'm having sex with a man, and it's for sex work, my mind focuses on the fact that this is a business with which I benefit and help benefit others with that money. How to help my family, for example. On the other hand, when I have sex with a partner with whom I am in an emotional relationship, there is only romantic love and the desire to make the person I love happy while he makes me happy too.

However, I have to admit that romantic love is the most difficult to achieve. Why does love hurt? I still haven't answered it. Maybe it's because I'm still so young. As I write this book and analyze love as a couple, I realize that despite everything I have experienced, I am only 28 years old. I still haven't reached the wisdom that the years have given me. Like the wisdom of my maternal grandfather or the wisdom of my paternal grandmother.

I didn't charge much for oral sex. Between $20 and 40 dollars. For a beginner, it was fine. At least it allowed me to get something to eat.

My first experience was oral. I neither liked nor disliked. I left my inner self going to another place, leaving only my mechanical body there, which had learned to do its task very well. Part of my good work was pretending it gave me pleasure, too. But it was all a perfect performance. Clients got what they were looking for, and I got the money. I never judged what I was pushed to do to survive. There is an actress, I am on stage, and the client is the audience enjoying the show—both parts are engaged in the present moment as if life might end at any time.

I lived intermittently between the street and my paternal grandmother's house. That tiny studio apartment housed the three of us. I learned that a good place to get customers was where the truckers parked. Service stations are among them. They were good to me. Truckers paid well for my oral sex, but others didn't want it. The others wanted to help me without me doing a sexual transaction, and they bought me food and gave me money generously. I think they saw I was just a kid. They must have imagined that my life was much more difficult than theirs, and they felt compassion for me.

The Flood That Drowned My Dream Job

*"... we must take the current when it serves
or lose our ventures."*

— William Shakespeare
1564 - 1616
English playwright, poet, and actor

The last job I had in Nashville, Tennessee, I was 16. I found it when I was on Craigslist looking for a job. They were looking for a store manager, and I felt they were talking to me. I thought it was the perfect position for me. I applied, I was interviewed, and they hired me right away. I worked there as a clothing store supervisor. Even though I later regretted it, during my rough young survivor years, I would go into clothing stores and steal something to help me get dressed.

It seemed like a miracle to me that they hired me to work there in the same store where I had previously stolen some little things when I told them that I had always chosen to go to that store because I loved their clothes.

Of course, they never knew or would have imagined that I had stolen from them. In my spirit, I asked for forgiveness, and I believe that a way to indirectly redeem and pay for what I took without permission has been that when I began to do well financially, I used a lot of my income to help others who were still living impoverished and marginality.

The manager loved me. He appreciated that I was well organized, reliable, and a good employee. That inspired me to devote myself more enthusiastically to generating sales and coordinating the employees under my supervision.

In that clothing store, I could find my style of dress, and I could buy what I needed without having to steal anymore. Which made me feel proud of my behavior and my achievements.

Everything was perfect there for me. There was no discrimination, and I evolved as a supervisor and as a person. I was immersed in a seasonal job. A calendar from November to January, when we sold all kinds of products.

I had shown remarkable efficiency in my position and for the calendar for two months, where I made an

$18,000 sale. However, as a store manager, there were times when the human resources department did not pay the employees and me, the money we signed through the contract. One day, when I was taking all the money to make all the deposits to the bank, that was a time when one of my employees was paid twice.

Unfortunately, this well-deserved paradise lasted only about six months. My dream then succumbed to the terrible flood that occurred in 2010 in Nashville, Tennessee, when the entire shopping center was flooded. I believe those fish in an aquarium who began swimming freely were saved.

On May 1, 2010, Nashville was brought to its knees, and many lives and homes were ruined. All imaginable rainfall records were broken. Thousands of properties were severely damaged or destroyed by the flood, and people were rescued from their homes and taken to shelters.

The Cumberland River had risen downtown to 51.86 feet on May 3. Nothing like it had been recorded since the early 1960s.

The flooding inundated the large Opry Mills and left the stores submerged in up to 10 feet of murky

water, and the place was closed for almost two years—
consequently, my dream job was also drowned.

I always loved rainy days. They seem to be a
blessing from heaven to feed all beings that live in
nature. So, every time it rained, I felt happy. However, in
my 16 years, I learned that even wise nature commits its
excesses. And that excess rain of 2010 drowned out
many dreams in the lives of Nashville people besides
mine.

So, I had to go back to sex work, even though I
had gotten used to making a living in another way.

I returned to the places where I already knew
there would be good customers and returned to offer
myself to the truckers. They were not into drugs or other
strange things. They simply sought instant gratification
to relax from their long hours of driving, days and
nights. They are not used to brutalizing sex workers;
therefore, a clientele ensures one would not be beaten
or killed.

The truckers always treated me well. Nor did they
make me feel any contempt for being a transgender
woman. And more than once, they gave me money
without me offering them any sex work in return. Good

people. Some already knew me, and when they saw me, I was like a friend from the road. I used to walk between the long-distance double-trailer trucks. Sometimes I was invited into truck cabins to have more private sex with the trucker. Oh, those cabins were more comfortable than the places where I sometimes lived.

I knew how to make good use of my purely feminine features. I was soft and, at the same time, passionate. Something that the men with whom I did my sex work liked a lot. Actually, I wasn't faking anything. I was just expressing my genuine femininity.

I always wore women's clothing, not only because I loved it, but also because it was the only way it would be easier for me to earn the money I needed.

When I officially started dressing as a girl, I was around 14 years old, even though by 13, I was fighting all the time to look like a girl. I would sneak my sister's clothes on my mother's side and go out dressed like that when no one in my family could see me.

I liked to feel my body tight in the tight clothes and notice how that tight top accentuated my small natural tits on my torso. I put on makeup with touches of naturalness because I didn't like to see myself wearing makeup like a carnival caricature.

Even though I was somehow pushed into sex work to survive, I always tried to take care of my body. I never drank alcohol or drugs, either. The most I tried once in a while had been marijuana, but I didn't want to do it often. Just sometimes.

Then, at age 17, I applied for a retail job at a gas station and convenience store in Nashville, Tennessee, and they hired me. I was first hired as a cashier. When the manager saw that I was doing an impressive job efficiently running that, he offered me a tiny raise as an incentive. But it wasn't enough for me.

First, I worked with excellence because I always liked being excellent in everything I did. And second, I needed to improve my lifestyle and get myself out of poverty. I needed to eat, dress, and feel better about myself. And I also liked the idea that I didn't need to do any sex work to make a living.

When I asked for a raise, he asked me how much I had to live on. I did my math, and I told him $35,000. He looked me up and down, offered me $30,000, and said that after a trial period, he would see if he could give me more. After my training, where I worked very efficiently, I would likely be promoted to manager of that branch as there was no one there.

He gave me more responsibilities and put me in charge of an additional store that was in total chaos. The cabinets were all out of order, the merchandise was everywhere, and much of it was outdated.

I had to work more than the hours I was paid for because it was an impossible place. The disorder would not have allowed customers to feel comfortable entering that store. But I didn't mind the excess work, I just wanted the place to look better, so I could work better and offer a better service to those who go there to buy something.

As it was a two-pump store located just off the highway, most clients were travelers, truck drivers, and tourists. One day, around three in the morning, some thugs broke into the store. He had thrown a brick through the door, and they reached in, turned the knob, went into the store, and the only thing stolen was 20 cartons of cigarettes. When I arrived, the police were already there.

I ended up managing two different stores at the same time. And it was time for my raise.

When I went to see the manager, who promised to give me $35,000 after my trial period, I asked him to give me the remaining $5,000. His response was that he would only give me a $1 raise, and for me to get the $5,000, I would have to give him oral sex. I looked at him with disgust. I had worked hard for a long time, and I had well organized the two stores for him, I had earned a decent salary, and all for that miserable pig to ask me for oral sex?

I quit right then and there. He stayed protesting because I was leaving him without replacements, but I went out with my head held high, searching for new horizons.

It was then that I decided to move to Atlanta, Georgia. It was January 1, 2014. I remember it very well because it was like a before and after of the transgender girl who had been born in Nashville, survived death after a violent and ungodly triple rape, and had been initiated into sex work in my late 14 years.

2

Atlanta, Georgia

"I have a dream that one day on the red hills of Georgia,
the sons of former slaves
and the sons of former slave owners
will be able to sit together at the table of brotherhood."

— Martin Luther King, Jr.
1929 - 1968
American Baptist minister and activist

Tennessee to Georgia

"Yesterday, I was clever,
so, I wanted to change the world.
Today I am wise, so I am changing myself."

— Rumi
1207 - 1273
Persian poet and Sufi mystic

 was 18 years old when I moved to Atlanta, Georgia. My whole purpose for going to Georgia was so that the family didn't care about me, and I would be able to plan my rebirth. My physical rebirth in the body of the woman.

When I was thirteen years old, and in my desire to develop my female body, I used to go to my sister's room and take some of her birth control pills. But I realized that this was not the way. I needed a more definitive resolution. So, I had to wait for the right age and financial opportunity to start hormone therapy.

I didn't know anyone in Georgia, and it was a good opportunity to start my life from scratch. It was a plan to be reborn and do everything on my own without having to look at the disapproving faces of others.

When I arrived in Atlanta, I looked to stay as a roommate since I didn't have all the money to rent an apartment. I met a guy who agreed to charge me a respectable sum, and I slept on the sofa in his living room.

Suddenly, one day, he started asking me for more and more money, only to sleep on that sofa in the living room. I refused and asked him to return the deposit I paid because that was not our agreement. However, he went to the police instead of paying me back, and they charged me. I ended up in jail in Georgia for thirty days.

In that jail where I had been put, I was exposed to an open population of inmates, and the jailers were the first to discriminate against me. They didn't give me a uniform or let me take a shower.

It came the time one day when I had no other choice but to defend myself but to fight back against a guard. Then, two came hard, beat me down, and broke my teeth.

I was so finished, angry, sad, and disappointed. After serving 30 days, I was able to get out on parole, and I had to go to court because I was facing a crime that would not help me in my purpose of improving my life. I lived immersed in terrible nights of stress, insomnia, fear, and panic during all that anguished process in which I was forced to live. And all because I didn't want to accept that the guy claimed to me that I increased his pay and, moreover, I ended up in jail because he fabricated criminal charges against me.

I was terrified because, during this time, I had received medication to treat my anxiety. I was going through a lot and needed to be able to sleep. So, the doctor prescribed pills to calm me down, but every time I went to see the probation officer for a urine drug test, it always returned positive for marijuana.

Fortunately, I got a letter from my doctor saying it would be a false positive because I'm taking pills he prescribed for my anxiety.

Those times were great torture for me. My whole plan to improve my life and go toward creating my true identity as a woman seemed to be falling apart. There were days that I just wanted to sleep or disappear from the hostility of the world that did not give me the place to be myself.

My experience of 30 days in jail, harassed by discriminatory threats from the jailers and some inmates, kept me up at night. At night, I doubted if my eyes would see the sunlight the next day. Danger hovered around me and lurked all the time. Not only the real danger, but the imaginary danger of expecting the worst amid those eternal 30 days of confinement.

Later, the interviews with the parole supervisor were not an easy task. It seemed that at any moment, he would stop me from finishing my probation properly and send me back to prison for tormenting my vulnerable self over and over again. Where did compassion go in this world? Where are the humanitarians? I was only a black transgender woman looking to create a decent life. Why this seemed to be impossible?

Finally, I was exonerated of my misdemeanor in Georgia. I paid for my papers to come out, and I was able to do it to speed up that process that would once again open the doors to my freedom. The freedom to return to the path you had started—the path to becoming TS Cindii, a woman.

I wanted to work, have a roof over my head, feed myself, and dress well. Feel happy with me. I was about to enter a territory where everything was different. Different regulations, different policies, different people.

I felt that Georgia could become my home.

In my search to earn money to rent a place, eat and dress, I went on Craigslist to see all the job postings there. And I saw one that I loved and applied for immediately. They were looking for a private detective and wanted to hire people who were not working, so they could dedicate themselves full time to the investigation. That's when I thought to myself, "Oh my God, that's me, a private detective." Even though I had no experience, I still tried.

I wanted to become a private detective. I was always good at research, passionate about analyzing everything, and, above all, I navigated the underground worlds and survived them. I was a street-smart girl with a gifted "charisma."

I applied immediately, and after passing several interviews and having my records checked and fingerprinted, I was hired. That's how my first job in

Georgia was as a private detective in a private company. I had to apply with my birth name: a male name, my father's.

It was a job that suited me perfectly because I was always neat, efficient, and very analytical. I loved researching and was very well-liked by those who interviewed me for this position. As soon as I was hired, I received 70 hours of training. Part of the training was the use of a firearm and some self-defense.

The cases I had to investigate were workers' compensation for slips and falls, infidelity accidents, and people needing to renew their SS or disability check. In cases of investigating infidelity, I would be in the car with tinted windows, following up on those who were suspected of being unfaithful. It was kind of fun. I felt like the protagonist of a movie zooming in and zooming out with my camera and sneaking into hotels or restaurants perfectly dressed to go unnoticed by those who I had to report about their unfaithful activities or not.

Once, I was investigating someone who seemed unfaithful to her partner.

I didn't like it when one day I noticed that the woman who had her head covered by a scarf and wore big dark glasses, when she entered a car where a man was waiting for her, she took off her scarf and her glasses and I could see that she had her bruised face. He hugs her, and she cries inconsolably on his shoulder. Then he started the car, and I followed them and saw they went into a motel in room 12.

I spent two hours waiting for them to come out while I had taken my computer to work on my report. After that time, I noticed that only he left the motel, looked everywhere, got into his car, and drove away.

I stayed there to see if she would come out too, but it then got dark, and she continued in the room. I made enormous efforts not to fall asleep. I walked into the motel lobby and poured myself several coffees, many times.

Finally, at about ten o'clock in the morning, I saw the maid knocked on the door and enter. I heard a scream, and immediately the police came. I walked over and presented my credentials and the photos of the guy who had taken her to that motel. It was later discovered that her alleged lover had been someone her partner had sent to pretend to love her and then kill her.

Thanks to the fact that I had been there investigating, it was possible to solve the crime that otherwise would have been difficult to reveal who the murderers had been.

After my successful work in that company of private investigators, a CIA claims agency contacted me where instead of earning $15 an hour, they would pay me $25. This new job was a qualitative leap in my working life. I worked in that CIA agency for almost a year. I was happy doing something positive for myself and for the community, while earning good enough money to improve my lifestyle.

I took advantage of that time of job and financial boom to begin the transition of my name change. When I lived in Tennessee, people in my family still called me by my birth name, which was my father's name. How could a woman feel fulfilled being called by a male name?

When I started hormone therapy in Atlanta, Georgia, I had to go to a website to buy them because the doctors wouldn't give them to me. I bought hormones on a black-market website because the doctors wouldn't give them to me without doing the therapy.

However, I then needed the doctors to prescribe me some spironolactone to reduce testosterone and flow while taking the estrogen, so my body would make more estrogen instead of testosterone.

I had started my hormone treatments, and the femininity results began to be evident in my physical body. When I started taking my hormone treatment in Georgia, getting my injection into my muscle was challenging and scary.

At a young age and having researched my path to being a whole woman on the outside, I couldn't wait to get my hormone treatment. But you cannot receive estrogen until you take hormone blockers for a year. I was looking forward to receiving hormones and the surgery to show the world who I was, finally—a woman.

I was going through various emotional emotions in my physical transformation process. It was trying to stick me, which felt like a self-inflicted punishment— desperate torture. I constantly screamed and cried. It was all I could do. It was too much to go through in a short time.

The treatment with spironolactone made me feel like menopausal sensations: sweats and sore nipples. My breasts hurt. It was like tightening a small knot. Although it was too painful, it was supposed to be pulled. I did all the homework and overcame the excruciating pains.

I went through all that to sculpt my female body. That is why one day, when I visited an art museum and saw the female sculptures, I wondered if the marble would have felt pain too when the artist's chisel hit it and chiseled it to, as Michelangelo said, *"I discover the statue that was hidden in the stone."*

I dressed as a woman most of the time, although to go to the offices of the investigative agency, I wore neutral clothes. It is always more convenient for a private investigator not to have a very conspicuous appearance. Even during my manicure, my nails were always pristine, sporting natural-toned colors.

I did the paperwork to change my name and got approval from the state of Georgia to do so. I was providing my new documentation to the CIA agent; they did not want to change my name on the card and put the new one. I had to keep my old identity or leave if I stayed with them. It hurt me deeply to receive that answer. Why was I denied the right to formalize my identity as a woman if I have always been one in my heart? Not only had I started hormone treatments, but I wanted to take myself seriously and change my name to reflect my true identity.

Unfortunately, given the CIA agent's refusal to acknowledge my new identity, I had no choice but to resign. I couldn't let this long and painful journey towards becoming a whole woman be sabotaged. I wouldn't take it, not even for the best job in the world. So, I quit.

I did not resign in an act of pride but to respect everything I had done to finally be recognized as the woman I had always been since my birth.

I thought about where my next physical transition step would be, and the answer came to me one day when a trans friend I had met in Georgia called me from New York. By then, I had saved enough money to go to New York without having to do sex work.

I got in my car, loaded my luggage and my dreams with it, and drove from Atlanta to New York. The direct trip would be about 17 hours, but I put more because I wanted to go through Nashville, Tennessee, to say hello to my parents and give them some money. By then, my mother and father had understood that my desire to see myself as a woman had never been a whim, nor was it a choice; it had been simply because I always felt like a woman. It relieved my soul a lot to receive that understanding from my parents.

While I was there, I wanted to bring flowers to the graves of my maternal and paternal grandparents. I knew that wherever they were, they would be giving me their support, the unconditional love that they always gave me when they were alive.

I walked through the cemetery, wondering if all those souls would have found relief from their sorrows in the universe where divine goodness dwells. Where the love that heals everything dwells. I couldn't help the tears running down my cheeks, but it was fine. Those tears were also washing away my pain. The pain that Tennessee made me feel with its intolerance, insults, and violent aggression towards my tender life as a child.

When I was leaving the cemetery, walking slowly and immersed in my feelings of goodbye to my grandparents, I felt a gentle perfumed breeze caressing my face. I knew that they were accompanying me from wherever they were, protecting me from the possible dangers my new journey could challenge me to face. Since then, whenever something makes me uneasy or a feeling of the danger stalking me, I evoke that moment, I evoke the caress of that breeze and that delicate perfume, and I feel secure.

My Transitional Journey

"The journey I'm taking is inside me.
Just like blood travels down veins,
what I'm seeing is my inner self,
and what seems threatening is just the echo
of the fear in my heart."

— Haruki Murakami
Japanese writer

To me, "Assigned Sex at Birth" doesn't feel the same as "Biological Sex."

I learned to forge my identity while developing my self-awareness when I discovered that my identity was a process I couldn't stop, nor was a choice. It was the sum of my character, perception, and world experience. It was a process of self-knowledge, which takes a lifetime and is in permanent dialogue with the other, with the findings that I discovered and continue to find out in private.

Even when I know who I am, like every human being, in the depths of consciousness, we all ask ourselves: Who am I?

What is defined as identity is gender, understanding this as the relationship we have with our sexuality and the sociocultural processes through which we could recognize ourselves as masculine or feminine. Gender manifests cultural traits: roles, conventions, and historical conditioning. So, I learned that identity and gender appeal to a person's integral perception of myself. The gender one feels as their authentic self may or may not coincide with the sex assigned at birth.

So, when science refers to "biological sex" to say the same thing as "sex assigned at birth," I understand that IT IS NOT THE SAME. Because I feel that biology, treated as a physical body, should not be divided and separated, from the psychology of the self, from sensations and the emotions of the body, does it mean then those emotions are not a product of biological processes? Why should they be separated?

I accept the "sex assigned at birth" because this is a "perception of someone external" to what he observes of the fissile physical body. It is a "label" that someone (the outside observer) puts on the child at birth. But I believe that my "biological sex" has been female, at least from the biology of my physical and emotional sensations.

Even when I didn't fully understand what was happening to me, from a very young age, I thought that one day I would wake up, and my body would be like my sisters. Then everyone would be happy, and so would I. No one would reject me. No one would look at me sideways. No one would gossip behind my back. My parents would hug me, and everyone would hug me. Oh, how much she had needed and wanted to be EMBRACED, accepted, loved.

One day, I spoke with a conservative adult and told him that I needed money to enter the transition. Bitterly, I heard her say, "Marry and mingle with the normal. Believe me; it will all go away. Youngsters like you don't have to do that. You don't have a clue of who you are. Get it out of your head." I lowered my head. I realized that I would waste my time and energy trying to persuade this person that no matter what I did, "my gender identity" would never go away.

I knew that choosing the path of manifesting my genuine inner self was the most challenging, the most dangerous, and the one with the most significant risk of being killed and mistreated. Despite all this, I chose to be faithful to who I am: a woman trapped in the body of a man.

Even though there is still a long way to go, and thanks to the courage with which we have faced disastrous social adversity, essential changes are being achieved.

I have friends in England who have dared to come dressed as a transgender woman at the police station and even educate police officers on how to help prevent and combat transphobic hate crimes.

I started transitioning when I was 13 ... although it is a never-ending process. Although, I began my transition when I was born with an assigned sex different from who I am.

The transgender people I met shared with me a variety of transition experiences. Some decided just to make a social transition. Others included making the legal and medical transition. And some chose not to do any of this to economic lack or fear of the results.

It takes enormous courage to accept yourself fully. I had to go through all the dark periods of the process. However, despite the dark doubts and fears, I decided to emerge into the light and embrace my entire feminine being. To physically embrace my identity as a woman.

I wanted to do it to honor the girl in me who had been so abused by societal transgender phobia. I wanted to do it, even if she was going to die trying. Because if I had to keep my woman self-trapped in a man's body, it would have been the same as living as a dead woman.

When I was 13 years old, the transition began with the decision to express my awareness of being a woman. Still, even as a child, I knew that my path was to show myself as a woman. I already wanted to be treated and respected for the gender identity I had undoubtedly assumed from a very early age. It was not easy to embark on the process of changing the way people saw me and how I felt inside.

I knew that the transition could mean many different things: medical treatment and hormones, changing my name and pronouns, changing my appearance and clothing, and announcing myself in society as the woman I am and always was, even though my body had not yet accompanied me in this personal mission. I knew that the process could be lengthy and expensive, with risks as well. However, I chose to pursue my inner calling. And there I went. And here I am.

I looked at myself in the mirror and projected a work of female transformation. I wanted to sculpt the best sculpture of myself as a tribute to compensate me for so much suffering and physical and emotional degradation. I felt how an artist might feel, expressing the talented inner work manifested outside in a sculpture.

I visited art museums. I needed to breathe the talent of sentient beings. The talent is reflected in their works of art, with an imagination immortalized by its beauty.

I owed myself the undertaking of reconstructing my physical appearance, which had been built since birth in the deep consciousness of my inner self. Rebuild what society tried so many times to destroy: the transgender woman in me.

I worked hard, raised money, and underwent the necessary surgeries that would sculpt me into a feminine body, a feminine face.

I went through all phases of the transition, from social to medical. They all cost me a lot. I began to present my feminine appearance according to my gender identity.

I immersed myself in hormone therapy to develop my feminine characteristics, like making my body hair disappear and distributing body fat towards my hips and breasts.

I further enhanced my breasts with natural-looking implants and had an orchiectomy to remove my testicles. I had my 'Adam's apple removed and facial feminization surgery to create more minor, feminine facial features.

Yes, it has been a long and arduous journey, but it was worth all the sacrifices I had to make to achieve my female body.

But regardless of whether and how a transgender person chooses to transition, they are no more "real" than other trans people who don't transition.

Someone's gender identity should always be respected, regardless of how they transition socially or medically.

3

New York

*"Make your mark in New York,
and you are a made man."*

— Mark Twain
1835 - 1910
American writer

New York:
Dreams and Nightmares

"Your heart knows the way. Run in that direction."

— Rumi
1207 - 1273
Persian poet and Sufi mystic

I was 24 when I moved to New York, carrying a bag full of dreams. I imagined that I could even act on Broadway. I had sung before at music events in Nashville. I had the voice, the talent to perform any character. Why not? There are hundreds of Cinderella stories, and they all end with a happy ending. Is it too much to ask after going through so much suffering, emotional and physical pain, all my life?

I pictured myself singing in a piano jazz bar in Soho, songs made famous by Ella Fitzgerald. Attend improvisation classes in contemporary dance. Take acting classes too. I've always been good on stage. Yes, all that and much more was what I dreamed of achieving in New York.

One of my dreams was to walk down 5th Avenue and Park Avenue, embracing Manhattan's streets with loving steps. Sat in Central Park, and the police walking past me would not harass me for being a black transgender woman. My dreams would continue with planning surgery to finally sculpt the woman's body that I longed to manifest to the world.

I went forward with my physical transition when I moved to New York. Georgia had been my legal transition and hormone treatments.

When I arrived in New York on June 29, 2017, I began planning the surgeries that would sculpt the woman within me into my body.

Fortunately, Medicare health insurance in New York State covered all the surgeries necessary to accomplish this purpose. I didn't have to take any money out of my pocket to do it, and I felt that all of it had been a blessing.

The first surgery was a breast augmentation. I really needed them because I was tired of putting on fake breasts and pretending they were mine when I was dressed. Then I had surgery to enhance my buttocks. I needed my curvaceous and very feminine body. For this, my hip was also worked on. The surgeries worked their magic, and my health insurance worked its miracle too. Otherwise, I would never have been able to raise all the money necessary to make my body that of a woman.

I was in my second marriage by the time of my surgeries, from which I received severe domestic violence. He always got drunk and wanted to fight.

On the day of the surgery, when my testicles were removed, I was up all night because we were arguing, going back and forth. At 6:00 am, I underwent surgery in a state of exhaustion. After they discharged me, around 11, he fought me when I got home. I was still under the effects of postoperative physical trauma and trying to heal the pain I felt from removing my testicles.

While I was recovering from surgeries, I was abused by my violent and alcoholic husband. I loved him. I knew he did too. However, he couldn't hold back his violent behavior when drunk and didn't want to treat himself to alcohol addiction. Finally, one day, I gathered courage and abandoned him. It was that painful decision, or if I didn't, I could end up beaten to death by him, stabbed, or thrown out the window.

I couldn't let my life come to an end that way. I had learned to love myself, to respect myself. He had learned to heal the deep wounds of the past. It seems that I had healed the trauma caused by the triple rape and the attempted murder.

Shortly after, I underwent facial surgery where my Adam apple was removed, my square chin disappeared, my nose was redone, my cheekbones were optimized, and with a general refinement of my features, I achieved a woman's face, beautiful and feminine. I also lifted my forehead shaved eyebrow, and my hairline pulled forward.

I felt enormous happiness when I noticed that my facial features softened after the surgery. I saw myself as feminine and had always felt in my inner being.

After hormone treatment and having my testicles removed, my voice also sounded more feminine. The echo of my inner woman resonated outside as I was, as I had always been: A WOMAN.

Now she could see me and be seen and heard as a full woman. I had already legally changed my name in Georgia, and now New York allowed me to achieve everything I needed to complete my womanhood.

The transformation was painful and taught me much about myself and my body. The journey toward becoming Candii was a struggle and worth trying it. It was a struggle not only in the process of sculpting my body into that of a woman, but also in repelling a law that had been implemented in 1977.

When I started to be an activist to turn an unjust law into a humanitarian resolution for transgender people, I realized that I was shining. Why would it shine? What would give my life that halo, that radiance? I realized that the glow emanated from my inner self-realized being on my outer self, finally, after so much sacrifice.

Even when I was very stressed, I smiled. Even when my physical wounds hurt, I smiled. Even when my affective life was threatened by dangerous violence, I went out into the street and smiled. During times of activism, I also smiled. I learned that smiles mask physical or emotional pain and help open doors. Who wants to be with a sad person? And I needed to have active participation in the world. I had to be part of a humanist movement that would alleviate the suffering of transgender people.

I immersed myself in getting that law changed. I organized many people and worked for organizations that didn't pay me. But I still continued. I had no money, but I still carried on. I had no one to talk to, but I continued anyway.

I still have terrifying and recurring nightmares where I am being chased and have to run for my life. I fled down dank, slippery, dark alleys. I climbed terraces and jumped walls. No matter how hard I tried to save myself, I felt that danger was always lurking around me, and I woke up drenched in sweat and with palpitations.

In my recurring nightmares, I used to walk at night looking for a way out and always ended up walking down a street where there were men with dark aspects. I knew that if I went near them, they would harm me. It had already happened in real life. Therefore, my terror was enormous. I didn't want to go through physical torment again. In one of those nightmares, while a threatening danger approached me, a black man wearing a white tunic arrived and told me to put on the light blue shoes he offered me. When I put on those shoes, I began to float and fly over those beings trying to harm me. I was beyond the reach of evil. However, something unexpected happened. From my higher level, I saw myself pouring compassion on those beings of darkness. Immediately, the danger disappeared, and those people received "human recognition." I woke up feeling relieved. Since then, that recurring nightmare has been resolved. I never experienced it again. And the fear, that terrifying fear that accompanied me everywhere, gradually dissolved to become courage.

Suddenly one day, all that poison that I masked with a smile that opened doors came to pass the bill. Suddenly, I started to feel worse and worse. An intense and growing pain stabbed me in the lower part of my belly. Or at least, I felt it there. As I could, I went to the hospital for what, I thought, was a severe stomachache. It was so intense that I couldn't even breathe.

They kept me on the hospital floor for eternity as my pain increased, and I writhed and screamed at that height. Finally, when they decided to treat me, they did an ultrasound and discovered that I needed emergency surgery because I was about to die from my peritonitis. My appendix was about to burst.

In October 2021, the day before the 42nd Sex Workers March in New York State, I was recovering in the hospital. As soon as I left, I went to look for a dress because I wanted to go to the event, but I didn't find anything. I finally went home and put on some nice outfits I had.

Even with the pain of the appendix surgery, I attended the event and did my part. When they found out that I had had an emergency operation for my peritonitis, they wanted to make arrangements, but I decided that nothing should be interrupted. We had worked so hard to achieve it that I couldn't allow it to be suspended or for me not to attend.

Over the years, I learned to heal my wounded self. My physical body survived all the ravages of life. It was not easy, and many times I could have died trying to live the life of my authentic self. Die from suicide attempts. Die from being assassinated.

As my healthier awareness began to emerge from the tragedies I had been through, I began to look for ways to heal my wounded self. To my wounded body. To my wounded mind. To my wounded spirit.

I had always loved expressing myself through dance and had the joy of meeting Anna, a transgender dance therapist I found at a music festival. She was giving a weekend workshop, and I immersed myself in it.

Although I had experienced joy when I danced before, this time, the dance had a consciously therapeutic purpose. It was like a luminous path towards producing self-conscious well-being. That path led me to practice yoga and meditation, something refreshingly healing that I do early every morning.

I used to be in music organizing events and also as a tour bus guide. I always liked to sing and be part of the church choir I led in ninth grade in high school. I was one of Glen Cliff High School's halftime team captains. I was fascinated by manifesting myself through dance and song. I still love it today; it does me good. It makes me feel alive.

Surviving Hellish Shelters in New York

"When it comes to luck, make your own."
— Bruce Springsteen
American singer, songwriter, and musician

I once heard a saying: *"if you don't succeed, you better be lucky."* So, I thought about how to succeed by living against the most adverse impediments that "forbid" me to be me.

It was forbidden to BE ME, but "it was against the law." Why would it be a crime to incarnate the true identity that I always felt in me? I wasn't waiting "to be lucky," so I chose the path to claim the right to be me actively.

Before I left Atlanta, Georgia, I made a list of things I wanted to take with me and things I would give away. I packed everything impeccably and was on my way. The trip to New York was a very long one since, in addition to passing through Tennessee, I stopped to rest in other states.

I drove several hours, happily looking not only at the landscapes but at the emotional journeys I had been through in my life and survived. I felt a mixture of pride in myself and the blessings I received from heaven, even in the most challenging times I had received.

I had no address in New York that I would go to. My heart only told me what a new destination was there. The transgender woman who had called me had mentioned something about a shelter, so as soon as I arrived, I contacted her and got the address of that place.

Upon my arrival, I said to myself, "Oh my God! Where did I arrive?" Fortunately, life has prepared me to face even the most adverse challenges. I would never have imagined that the shelter would be an "every man for himself" place.

I discovered that I had to tune into all my senses to survive that place. I began to learn the rules of the shelter rapidly. I knew what to avoid when to be invisible, and when to be visible.

Like animals of different species caged in the same place, the survival instinct was the first thing to be developed, or you would not wake up alive the next day. Or you will lose your few belongings.

I met one of my transgender sisters, who coached me on staying safe and being cautious when reacting to people who might want to have sex with me without me wanting it. Turning the rulers of that place against me would get me kicked out or break into my bedroom door and rape me. It was a lot to fight against to have the guarantee that, in that refuge, one would see the light of the sun the next day.

What was supposed to be a place to house the homeless destitute was sheer hell in the fight for survival. If someone desirable refuses to have sex, and their arbitrary rules are not followed, they would go to their computer, lock your room and throw your belongings out on the street. So, you must return to the main center, relocate, and find another shelter where the laws wouldn't be too different.

My New York nightmare was that I had to go through 13 different shelters. From the Bronx to Harlem, from there to Manhattan, until after much suffering, emotional torture, abuse, and uncertainty, I found my permanent home in Brooklyn.

Moving to the New York shelters taught me a lot. He taught me about many different types of drugs. He taught me about crystal meth. He taught me about cocaine. He taught me how people used to do it and shoot themselves. I've seen plenty of people overdosing in bathrooms. It was like a horror movie, and the security guys wanted to punish them.

Addicts engage in irrepressibly violent behavior. The risk of being raped in those places and even murdered was very high.

Many wanted to punish me just for *"being what you are,"* they told me. It was scary staying in a shelter. Where would I go? Under a bridge? Sneak into a train station? Live from boxcar to boxcar like depression-era vagrants?

It was sad to see that this place considered a "refuge" for the homeless was the shelter of terror, crime, drug abuse, rape, and murder.

I didn't want to do drugs, but I slightly tried. I did it so as not to be marginalized from the marginalized. If

I resisted their addictive behaviors, I would be perceived as an undercover law enforcement worker disguised as a homeless person. I would never do that. I would not expose those who fell into crime, not by choice, but because there was often no other alternative to survive.

When I started my life in New York, I was homeless. I was so used to being independent and living in unrestricted housing that the shelters in New York were oppressive with their strict regulations, while on the other hand, the crime levels were as high as in a high-security penitentiary.

I looked for a possible way out, and that was marriage.

I went to live with a man as if it had been a partnership. But since that "partnership" was not legally recognized in the state of New York, I got legally married the same month to a different man. It was a good idea, yes. The marriage rescued me from the rugged shelters, yes. Was it good to live with him? Nope.

When we met, I wasn't in love with him, but I liked him, and he was attracted to me. However, it takes more than attraction to live with someone and be at least somewhat happy or peaceful living under the same roof. But for me, there was neither peace nor happiness. There was also no romance—just strenuous sex.

Unfortunately, he drank and drank a lot. He was an alcohol addict. Sometimes the domestic violence reached levels where my life, once again, could be in danger.

The Abuse of Power

When I moved to New York, I was sentenced to give oral sex to a vice officer, or I would go to jail.

It all started when I got out of the building to smoke a cigarette in the street. Immediately, two vice officers appeared and harassed me with their intimidating approach. I knew I was in danger. I was in danger for being a black transgender woman. I was in danger at the hands of "law keepers" because they had the power to be their voice and not mine that would be heard.

One of them smugly told me that he was offering me $1,200 if I collaborated undercover as an informant, denouncing who were drug dealers and sex workers. I refused to do it. I did not accept something that humanly I would later regret. I couldn't cause more harm to those with enough pain in their helpless lives.

I could not live happily with myself if I had denounced many who, like me, have been marginalized from society and, consequently, have been pushed to practice any kind of illegal work to survive. I openly told them, "Do you think that sex workers are happy to expose their bodies to all kinds of abuse and even death at the hands of predators, serial killers, and transgender phobia? Not to mention all kinds of sexual deceased to which get treatments are almost impossible." They looked at each other, mucking a smile. Then, they told me, cornering me against the wall, that if I didn't do it, I had two options, suck their dick or go to jail.

I knew that going to jail for who knows how many charges against me, they could have been invented, and it was not what I was looking for in my life.

As a black transgender woman, I had been cautious not to end up in a penitentiary. It would have been a death sentence in a cell or a bathroom, not without being perversely sexually tortured. I knew that going to jail would be certain death. Once I was put behind bars, the risk of dying as a black transgender woman was sky-high. And if I didn't die, I would suffer horrendous torments, abuses, and rapes. If I came out unscathed, I would never be able to get a job and home. No one wants to give people who have been convicted work or housing opportunities.

I agreed to humiliate myself before those uniformed pigs. They escorted me into a parking garage, satisfying their wish to humiliate me by sucking on their disgusting members.

They left me at a crosswalk, where I crossed, relieved that I was no longer in a trap, and ran to the shelter. Although the relief, I was still in shock.

When I got back to my place, I was shaking. I learned that one does not get used to abuse, no matter how many times they have been repeated in life. When I entered, a friend who saw me arrive ran to hug me while I collapsed on the floor, bathed in tears.

Years later, I was arrested in Brooklyn in Brownsville after New York decriminalized marijuana. I was arrested because the courts had not yet removed any pending warrants. So, that was a flaw in the judicial system.

When I was arrested, there were five officers stopped around my vehicle. They then took me out of the car and chained me to a metal bench in the same area for 18 hours. The guard suggested with his hand that I stand up, turn around, and crouch down while my head was covered with a dress.

I had a temper of steel. You must be that way to survive the worst. It seemed that a part of my mind was preparing me to absorb high-stress levels and survive the mental and bodily damage it meant.

What you feel is a terrifying sense of vulnerability. No one knows how the life of someone caught by law enforcement officers in these highly discriminatory circumstances can end. Especially if the person arrested is black, and much worse if that black person is a transgender woman.

The Calling to Support Transgender People

"When injustice becomes law,
resistance becomes duty."

— Thomas Jefferson
1743 -1826
American statesman, Founding Father,
and the third President of the United States

With time and greater inner strength, I devoted myself
to supporting many organizations to encourage new
ventures, start-ups, and black-owned businesses
financially.

I found the internal and external resources to
facilitate the well-being of those who, like me, had been
seen in the abyss of marginality because the human
profile to which society had condemned them did not
correspond to what is expected of what is considered
"normal."

Things that mattered to us were always at risk,
especially for those of us who live with the deep
disruptions that occur in the world around trans people.
How to transcend adversity and constant dangers

without dying trying? It had been a question that I could only answer with: "BELIEVE IN YOURSELF."

Once, I have survived my 'dark night of the soul.' Going through the most primitive, threatening, and limiting places within myself and society, I could see a bright light emerging prosperous and expansive energy to embrace the dream of being me and breathe myself fully in freedom.

I knew those who rejected me would not accept me, but that no longer meant a barrier to embrace my true self; instead, it reinforced my courage to recognize my value. To bring it up to the scene of life as a role model for those who are still struggling, emerging from the degradation they've been condemned to stay.

I learned that the so-called "here and now" considers the present moment as eternity—the place where the divine of one's being, and the universe is found and manifested.

I embarked on my calling, as does the hero in the leadership's mission, to inspire those who have been abandoned in dehumanizing marginalization.

The battle against the darkness of society is sometimes demoralizing and deteriorating. However, there was a call to save my heart from hatred, resentments, grievances, suicide attempts. . . So many gloomy things.

When COVID first hit New York, I was part of the mutual aid black fund that doled over a million dollars. I helped distribute over $500,000 to the black and brown community that teaches and seeks sex work.

This is a time of hard-earned appreciation. It has been great learning for me to appreciate the struggle required to overcome challenges. To be reborn from the deadly blows of the road. I learned to appreciate the opportunities that arise to be resilient in times of great struggle or despair.

Together, we head towards the new possibilities that still await us and the adventures born from the tests we live.

Repealing
the Walking While Trans Ban

*"Just because they're not on your road
doesn't mean they've gotten lost."*

— Dalai Lama
Nobel Peace Prize, 1989

I spoke at the New York University School of
Law, where more than 700 lawyers were in
session when they were credited with the law
that was struck down. I openly shared that I had been
abused by two police officers who threatened to put me
in jail for the statute that has now been repealed.

I had led the "Repeal the Walking While Trans
Ban" in the hope that no one would have to suffer a
trauma like mine again, and I succeeded.

United in a humanitarian effort to obtain justice
aiming to repeal the "Walking While Trans" Ban, we all
together achieved that the bill would be approved.

The Committee on Lesbian, Gay, Bisexual,
Transgender, and Queer Rights, the Committee on Civil
Rights, the Committee on Criminal Justice Operations,

the Committee on Immigration and Nationality Law, and the Committee on Sex and Law of the New York City Bar Association were part of the project to support the freedom of previously criminalized people.

The City Bar Association, an organization of more than 24,000 attorneys and judges dedicated to improving the administration of justice, released the report supporting the proposed repeal of New York Penal Law § 240.37 to eliminate a criminal statute that has a disparate impact on lesbian, gay, bisexual, transgender, and queer ("LGBTQ") people and other vulnerable minorities.

New York state has repealed the so-called "walking while trans walking" ban. The bill was passed to repeal statute 240.37, which prohibited loitering for prostitution, from the state penal code. This law, unfortunately, had been used disproportionately against women of color and transgender women, in particular. The police used that law as a scary excuse to harass them just to get on with their days.

No one should be charged with prostitution simply for walking down the street. I felt thrilled. I've reached one of the stars of my missions in life.

February 2, 2021 was a miraculous day. It was when justice was served for the innocent and defenseless, often falsely criminalized just for walking down the street.

That day, New York Governor Andrew Cuomo signed legislation to repeal the state's anti-loitering law affecting trans women. So, that law was enacted to repeal a section of New York criminal law that promoted arbitrary and discriminatory policing of transgender women and cisgender women of color.

As founder and Executive Director of Black Trans Nation, I was then among the lawmakers who voted to repeal this law, and I said, "Repeal & seal the Walking While Trans Ban is a steppingstone to equality in the state of New York. We are walking into a new beginning. We are grateful our humanity is becoming acknowledged. We are beginning to unravel our existence outside the criminal justice system."

Section 240.37 of the New York criminal law, also known as the "walking while trans" ban, prohibited loitering for the purpose of engaging in a crime of prostitution. This law, dating from 1976, was intended to prohibit vagrancy for the purpose of prostitution.

However, it had been primarily used to target transgender and cisgender women of color, even when they had been law-abiding.

According to data from the New York State Division of Criminal Justice Services, it was shown that 91% of people arrested under the statute were black and Latino. Of these, 80% identified as women.

Fortunately, Senate Bill 1351 not only repealed section 240.37 but also amended section 230.01, which dealt with affirmative defenses to prostitution.

I was happy that the law had been repealed, and although our trauma will not go away, knowing that no one will be profiled or experience trauma like mine helps us to continue our healing process.

Enough work still needs to be done on our emotional and physical selves to remove the wounds caused by marginalization and to be treated as undesirable in the larger frameworks of society. With this stigma, it is already challenging, if not impossible, for us to get a decent job, study, and have the right to comprehensive education and health care.

The statute, dating from 1976, belonged to an era in which state officials approved policies aimed at "cleaning the streets."

As sad as it is to admit this, they have been and are dehumanizing excuses. It often meant using the imprisoned system to get black bodies out of spaces, even black bodies not involved in illegal activity, to make those spaces more attractive to tourists and white New Yorkers. This increased in the 1990s to weed out LGBTQ youth of color and drive out their presence in gentrifying neighborhoods. It was a justified raid under the umbrella of "cleaning the city of undesirables."

I was actively urging state legislators to pass legislation to protect sex workers in New York and repeal a loitering law known as the "Walking While Trans Ban." I did it during a rally at the State Capitol in June 2019, and that law was officially repealed.

How could I not be there encouraging this legal change that is so important for many trans women who, like me, had been victimized under the statute?

Two years earlier, my humiliation had occurred when two New York police officers arrested me under the pretext of 240.37 and forced me to perform oral sex on them. It was very traumatic for me not to have been able to report the incident because who would have believed a black transgender sex worker? When I finally made it public, I felt like a healing shower cleaned the awful experience I was forced to live.

The Healing Power of Art
Oh, Art! Such a safe place to grow!

*"Art washes away from the soul
the dust of everyday life."*

— Pablo Picasso
1881 - 1973
Spanish painter, sculptor, printmaker, ceramicist,
and theater designer

Intuitively, one day I felt that expressing myself through art liberated my being, which was chained to the pain produced by the intolerance of my environment and society in general.

The times I had the opportunity to perform on stage was a magnificent experience.

At this moment, writing my story here is a form of healing my mind and my spirit. It even heals my story, the trauma of my childhood, so that the terrifying ghosts of the past no longer haunt me.

Growing up, I had found a place where I could perform the artist in me. I used to participate in parades in Nashville, Tennessee, like the Tennessee State Homecoming parades, where I danced as part of a group of dancers. I also danced on Channel 3 in Tennessee; I danced in a church as part of a dance team led by Kirk Dewayne Franklin, an American choirmaster, gospel singer, dancer, songwriter, and author. He is best known for leading urban contemporary gospel choirs such as The Family, God's Property, and One Nation Crew (1NC), among many others.

I was excited to be part of the show business when I was younger. It seemed to me that being surrounded by artists made me feel safe. Their transcendent, expanded, and compassionate minds did not harbor discriminatory feelings towards anyone who manifested themselves as "different" from ordinary people. I felt alive, free, creative, and productive. I earned money and felt great for not being discriminated against.

Soon I've become directly involved in organizing numerous arts events outside of Hooters, at the Hard Rock Cafe, and even on a music tour bus in my 18 years.

Whenever I had the chance, I visited art museums and exhibitions.

I always felt attracted to sculptures, theatrical costumes, songs, music, and Broadway musicals, as if they were a creative force capable of manifesting our deep emotions.

I found in exploring psychodrama, movement therapy, and singing expressive techniques where my spirit found its voice, its presence, and was heard, where my body moved on stage and flowed, appreciated instead of judged or discriminated against.

I once read in a postcard what Tolstoy said about being creative, "Art is the activity by which a person, having experienced an emotion, intentionally transmits it to others." His words could not have been truer than what I feel when I receive an art manifestation or when I have an opportunity to practice it.

Art was a saving therapy—a cure to my deepest wounds, my abused soul violated by discrimination. Art allowed me to be healed, although the journey still needs more to receive.

When I admired the sculptures of renowned artists, I couldn't stop thinking about how much pain and dreams I had invested in sculpting my true female body, carved in my body born as a man. For those who have never felt the alienation of knowing that they are a person different from the sex assigned at birth, it will be tough, if not impossible, to understand what is suffered. It will be challenging to support that we must go through these traumatic and expensive surgical interventions because otherwise, it is like being buried alive. It is like being immobilized, without a voice, without caresses, in a rigid body that does not feel itself and will never touch because it was never felt like mine.

I also explored and continue to practice my holistic healing through yoga, meditation, movement therapy, and conscious eating. I seek that my body, mind, and spirit live in constant harmony.

My daily meditation and yoga start early in the morning. I love to begin my day, aware of my decisions, thoughts, and feelings. I care for who I am. I learned to take care of myself after going through the darkest corridors in the underworld and having survived the terror, the sadness, physical and emotional suffering, intolerance, violence, and death.

I encourage transgender people to find their path through peace in ways where their disturbed life would be relieved. A journey where forgiveness to ourselves, our family, and our general environment is highly therapeutic, as well as our commitment to preserving the self we feel, is us. I encourage attending support groups of any kind available for suicidal tendencies and addictions.

Practicing any form of therapeutic approach relieves the mind-body connection between what we've been told we were and what we genuinely feel we are.

I do not intend to change the world; I simply need the world not to want to change me to encapsulate me in a body and behavior that is not me.

Who Wants to Be a Sex Worker?
NO ONE
does it by a natural choice

"May your choices reflect your hopes, not your fears."

— Nelson Mandela
1918 - 2013
Nobel Peace Prize
The first President of South Africa

I wish that many sex workers could choose to live through their hopes, through their desires to integrate into society instead of being disintegrated from it.

I wish that many sex workers had never had to choose to be one because they had no other alternative to sustain their survival.

I hope societies are healed, compassionate, humanitarian, and tolerant towards those considered "different" or "undesirable."

People may ask why someone would want to be a sex worker.

The answer to that question is that THEY HAVE HAD NO OTHER OPTION BUT TO SURVIVE a hostile society that does not provide any human or humanitarian support so that transgender people are decently integrated into society instead of being terribly marginalized and expelled from it.

Discrimination, abuse, harassment, violence, and murder are experiences that transgender people usually suffer.

Many are not even aware that these sufferings begin in childhood. From an early age, they face the stigma, discrimination, and social rejection in their homes and communities for expressing their gender identity. Such discrimination, violence, and criminalization prevent transgender people from developing and receiving social benefits like any other human being. They are also prevented from being treated in health centers whenever needed.

Unfortunately, most people think that being transgender is a choice. No, at all. Being transgender IS NOT A CHOICE: IT IS the reality that a human being experiences in his feelings and sensations, knowing they are totally different from the sex assigned to them at birth.

A transgender person DID NOT CHOOSE TO BE. They were born different from what their bodies tell the world.

To make life more difficult for transgender people, society (often starting at home): EXCLUDES THEM. They try to disintegrate them instead of integrating them. Therefore, by not being able to be "integrated" into decent working conditions, by not being able to be "integrated" into renting a decent place to live, by not being "integrated" into their family environment, by not being "integrated" into education that allows them to evolve socially and personally, many transgenders are pushed to survive under the following conditions:

1. Homeless

2. Outlaw

3. Suicidal

4. Substance addicts to alienate them from the grief of not being able to be

5. Sex work

6. Outcasts

7. Homeless

8. No health protection or treatment

9. The above list becomes worse if the transgender person is black.

Transgender sex workers are more likely to experience violence and death than other sex workers. They are the ones who also have a much higher percentage of risk of contracting HIV than other adults.

Although bringing awareness and education to society to recognize transgender people as human beings instead of monsters, they are still being murdered for who they are.

Trans people are often misgendered by police or fail to report attacks. Therefore, it is difficult to know the totality of transgender women who have been brutally harassed and murdered.

Most of the deaths tend to happen to black trans women. Trans women of color are cruelly attacked and cannot petition because their work is considered illegal.

These laws that criminalize sex work force them to go underground, increasing the risk that their violence and deaths will be silenced by indifference, lack of compassion, and lack of justice for these human beings who have not been able to find another way of surviving than through sex work.

Those who contract the sex work of transgender women assume that they can attack, violate, rob, and even kill them since no one will ask for justice for them. These "clients" of sadistic behaviors take advantage of the terror that transgender sex workers experience. Even some law enforcement people often take advantage of their position to abuse them.

Even though being a sex worker is dangerous, whether you are trans, cis, LGBTQ, or straight, it is vastly more dangerous if the sex worker is a trans woman of color.

We don't even know about most of the violence that happens to our sisters. Most of the deaths occurred in black trans women. Trans women of color know what it's like to be attacked for who they are and not have anyone to turn to for help because their work is illegal.

Laws that criminalize sex work increase the growth of the underground industry, which is then punished and made more dangerous because those who are pushed into sex work have their voices silenced, their bodies violated, and their minds terrified.

Both law enforcement and civilians usually profile trans women of color as sex workers, even when they are not engaging in sex work.

Sex workers are easy targets, and highly vulnerable prey, especially if they are from a low-income community. They are routinely abused verbally, physically, or sexually. The violence that exists throughout the country.

Most trans or suspected trans sex workers were harassed, attacked, or abused by the police. Laws against sex work, especially against trans women of color, cause them to receive the greatest burden of violence and death. This situation was further exacerbated when online platforms and screening tools needed to screen customers, share this information with their sisters, and prevent attacks from vicious and hostile predators were banned.

Some transgender sex workers are seeking a firearms license to protect themselves. No transgender sex worker wants to react violently to the ungodly violence they receive and even the danger of being killed. However, many find no solution other than providing themselves with all kinds of weapons to defend themselves because they are always exposed to the possibility of something bad happening.

Transgender people have little to no chance of being employed like the opportunities that cis people have. There is great discrimination against transgender people, making it impossible for them to be hired in a legal job.

A vast majority of black trans people live in terrible destitution and face two very terrible things in society: Violence and Indifference. Which pushes them to total helplessness or to embark on dangerous sex work. Not for pleasure, just to survive. Just to live another day because it's uncertain if that transgender person will ever see the light of day after a very dark night.

Trans people do not have free access to education, they are rejected when applying for rent, and their way of eating is destitute. Adding to this high cost of their lives is the risk of being unable to be treated in the health systems, since discrimination there is also very high.

Sex as a means of survival is the abyss that black or Latina trans women are pushed into. At the bottom of that hole, only the echo of the torment of those who have been precipitated into that hell can be heard without "anyone from above" reaching out a hand to integrate them into the world of the "human beings" that they also are.

Transgender people cannot survive and thrive if they are constantly policed and criminalized, as trans women are more likely to be incarcerated than the general population.

Once imprisoned, esteem is higher. If a transgender sex worker survives the violent abuse and high chance of being murdered in jail, once they get out, they have absolutely no chance of being hired for legal work or accepted to rent somewhere they can live decently.

Due to legal discrimination, if our assigned sex at birth has been "male," then the law will put us in all-male jails and prisons. There, the risk of being violently abused and even killed is horribly higher.

I was one of the many transgender women of color who were pushed into sex work since I was a child as the only means of survival.

It's been a long time since I stopped doing it, but that's not why I've ignored the agony suffered by those who still work in sex. I have actively worked so that through my voice, trans women can be heard in a world that criminalizes them.

Decriminalizing sex work will help sex workers go out and earn money safely, take care of themselves, and have the option to change careers if they decide to do so one day.

It's essential for society to recognize that if sex workers exist, it is because there is a large market demanding sex services, and many in this market are "clean people" openly living in society.

The Right to Live and Be

"The people have a right to the truth
as they have a right to life,
liberty and the pursuit of happiness."

— Epictetus
AD 50 - 135
Greek Stoic philosopher

Being transgender does not mean suffering from a mental disorder. It cannot be "cured" with treatment. Nor is it a choice. It is what it is: a big difference between what is outside, the body, and what is being experienced inside, within the person's true self.

Transgender people are at high risk of societal violence and even death. The average life expectancy due to this terrible level of social intolerance is about 35 years.

A 2015 national survey on transgender discrimination found that 60% of health care providers refuse treatment for transgender people. Nearly 70% of transgender people surveyed had experienced physical or sexual violence at work. In addition, adolescents in schools are experiencing a high level of violence and sexual abuse.

Even kids are at risk.

Children who came out as transgender ended up verbally harassed, physically, and sexually assaulted because of their sexual identity.

Research cases indicate that 82% of transgender people have considered suicide, and 40% have attempted suicide. Suicidality is highest among transgender youth.

Among the factors that influence suicide in transgender youth are interpersonal and environmental aggression, internalized self-stigma and adverse childhood experiences, and not having the necessary support from family, school, and the environment that surrounds the child who already in her childhood felt transgender.

Cumulative negative stress emerges in the psyche of transgender youth who face the anxiety of living stalked by the imminent danger of receiving aggression, violence, rape, rejection, and even the risk of being killed. Therefore, it is highly probable that the suicidal tendency accompanies young transgender throughout their life if they have not had the opportunity to find a support group and the appropriate psychotherapeutic treatments.

Not only the social aggression to which they are exposed undermines the being of the transgender youth. The emotional and negligent abandonment by the family, the abandonment of their studies due to the harassment that they can easily receive at school, and the few opportunities to develop as valuable people in society, also push the young person to want to take their own life as the best means to alleviate their deep emotional pain.

Among the risk factors that drive transgender youth to seek their own death is knowing they are "unwanted" and repelled by their own family and school.

Transgender people have a higher prevalence of suicidal thoughts and attempts than others. Among those with lower socioeconomic status, i.e., less education, unemployed, lower family income, homeless, those experiencing severe psychological distress, report excessive consumption of alcohol and/or illicit drugs.

Many of these characteristics are associated with or are after-effects of exposure to stigma, discrimination, and violence.

Minority stressors, such as experiences of discrimination, family rejection, and stigma, are commonly reported and put transgender people at higher risk for suicidal thoughts and attempts.

Transgender people face discrimination, and due to penning in and being prevented from finding decent ways of life, the suicide rate among transgender people is high.

The Suicide Prevention Resource Center reports that more than 83% of transgender people had considered suicide, and 54% had attempted it.

The National Suicide Prevention Lifeline is 1-800-273-8255.

Awards and Honors

From my childhood in Tennessee until I arrived in New York, the journey route has been colored by all kinds of suffering. Emotional, psychic, and physical traumas that sculpted this transgender woman that I am proud to have achieved.

I am the product of my hard work, commitment to respect the true self that lives in me, and resilience to social hostility and family rejection early in my life.

I have survived the worst, although that does not mean that I do not have to continue to face the explicit or tacit violence of a society that is disinterested in the human needs of transgender people.

After great efforts, fears, torments, and struggle, I have achieved recognition and also awards for my mission of dedicating myself to defending the human rights of transgender people, especially transgender women of color.

The journey has been long; however, it was short. I started at 13, and now I'm just 29 years old. I hope to be able to continue because I know the life expectancy for us barely reaches 35 years in the best of cases.

I want to dedicate these Awards and Honors to those who have supported me unconditionally despite the fear, the danger, and the violence. Also, to people of "accepted society" who nurtured with remarkable humanitarian spirit had opened doors and platforms to allow our voice to be heard and succeed. To all those who encouraged the call to prevent us from being criminalized and who also continue to be active in the purpose of educating society so that they understand that a trans person is not like that by choice but because they are faithful to the essence they feel in her interior and different from the sex assigned to her at birth.

Manhattan Young Democrats
Young gets it done
Policy Advocate of the year 2020

1st Annual District 45
Women of Distinction Awards
CERTIFICATE OF DISTINCTION
Community Advocate

City Council Citation
Ts Candii
New York City Council 45th district
Farah Lewis
March 8, 2021

2021 as published in City & State Power of
Diversity Women 100
November 2021

Office of the president
Borough of Queens, City of New York
Citation of Honor
Ts Candii
Donouan Richards Jr.
President of the Borough of Queens
November 11, 2021

OFFICE OF THE PRESIDENT
BOROUGH OF BROOKLYN
CITY OF NEW YORK
Citation
TS Candii
Eric L. Adams
President of the Borough of Brooklyn

November 11, 2021
Gay city news
LGBT+ power players
June 2022

AMNY Politics NY Gay City News
LGBT+ power players
June 2022

Vanessa L. Gibson
President of the Borough of the Bronx Citation of Merit
Ts Candii
March 10, 2022

Vanessa L. Gibson
President of the Borough of the Bronx Citation of Merit
Black Trans Nation
June 15, 2022
Dans Paper & NGLCC
Out East End Impact awards
2022

New York State Assembly
Citation
Ts Candii
August 14, 2022
Rebecca A. Seawright
NYS ASSEMBLY 76 DISTRICT

Power Women of Queens
Schneps Media's Power Women
September 29, 2022

*"Life is Short.
Discrimination shouldn't shorten it."*

T.S. Candii
28 years old, September 2022

www.tscandii.com

Made in the USA
Middletown, DE
07 October 2022

11958417R00086